Cambridge School
Shakespeare

D0473138

1E TEMPEST

CAMBRIDGE
UNIVERSITY PRESS

Edited by Linzy Brady and David James
Series editors: Richard Andrews and Vicki Wienand
Founding editor: Rex Gibson
May 2014

CAMBRIDGE
UNIVERSITY PRESS

University Printing House, Cambridge CB2 8BS, United Kingdom

Cambridge University Press is part of the University of Cambridge

It furthers the University's mission by disseminating knowledge in the pursuit of education, learning and research at the highest international levels of excellence.

www.cambridge.org
Information on this title: www.cambridge.org/9781107615533

First published 1995
Second edition 2005
Third edition 2014

Printed in the United Kingdom by Latimer Trend

A catalogue record for this publication is available from the British Library

ISBN 978-1-107-61553-3 Paperback

Cover image: RSC/Swan Theatre 2011, © Donald Cooper/Photostage

Contents

Introduction

This *The Tempest* is part of the **Cambridge School Shakespeare** series. Like every other play in the series, it has been specially prepared to help all students in schools and colleges.

The **Cambridge School Shakespeare** *The Tempest* aims to be different. It invites you to lift the words from the page and to bring the play to life in your classroom, hall or drama studio. Through enjoyable and focused activities, you will increase your understanding of the play. Actors have created their different interpretations of the play over the centuries. Similarly, you are invited to make up your own mind about *The Tempest*, rather than having someone else's interpretation handed down to you.

Cambridge School Shakespeare does not offer you a cut-down or simplified version of the play. This is Shakespeare's language, filled with imaginative possibilities. You will find on every left-hand page: a summary of the action, an explanation of unfamiliar words, and a choice of activities on Shakespeare's stagecraft, characters, themes and language.

Between each act and in the pages at the end of the play, you will find notes, illustrations and activities. These will help to encourage reflection after every act, and give you insights into the background and context of the play as a whole.

This edition will be of value to you whether you are studying for an examination, reading for pleasure or thinking of putting on the play to entertain others. You can work on the activities on your own or in groups. Many of the activities suggest a particular group size, but don't be afraid to make up larger or smaller groups to suit your own purposes. Please don't think you have to do every activity: choose those that will help you most.

Although you are invited to treat *The Tempest* as a play, you don't need special dramatic or theatrical skills to do the activities. By choosing your activities, and by exploring and experimenting, you can make your own interpretations of Shakespeare's language, characters and stories.

Whatever you do, remember that Shakespeare wrote his plays to be acted, watched and enjoyed.

Rex Gibson
Founding editor

This new edition contains more photographs, more diversity and more supporting material than previous editions, whilst remaining true to Rex's original vision. Specifically, it contains more activities and commentary on stagecraft and writing about Shakespeare, to reflect contemporary interest. The glossary has been enlarged too. Finally, this edition aims to reflect the best teaching and learning possible, and to represent not only Shakespeare through the ages, but also the relevance and excitement of Shakespeare today.

Richard Andrews and Vicki Wienand
Series editors

This edition of *The Tempest* uses the text of the play established by David Lindley in **The New Cambridge Shakespeare**. Please note that the line numbers in this edition differ in places from those of the Cambridge School Shakespeare first edition.

The play begins with a storm at sea raised by the spirit Ariel on the orders of his master, the sorcerer Prospero – the former duke of Milan.

▲ A ship carrying Alonso, the king of Naples, his son and courtiers, is wrecked in the storm. In the confusion, they are separated and it is feared that the king has lost his only son.

▲ They are confused by their new surroundings on what seems to be a magic island. Two courtiers, one of them the king's brother, plan to murder him in order to take the crown on their return to Naples. What they do not know is that Prospero rules the island. Twelve years before, Prospero was overthrown as duke of Milan by his treacherous brother Antonio and Alonso.

Prospero's magic art gives him control over the island and over Ariel, who has been freed from a life of torment and now serves Prospero by carrying out his commands.

Prospero lives on the island with his daughter Miranda (left). Another inhabitant is Caliban, the son of a witch, who was born on the island. Prospero keeps Caliban in slavery for attempting to assault Miranda, but Caliban accuses Prospero of stealing the island from him. He thinks of himself as the rightful owner.

▶ Prospero devises plans to confront Alonso and Antonio with the wrong they did to him. He also arranges for the king's son, Ferdinand (pictured), to make it safely to shore and to meet Miranda.

▼ They fall in love at first sight, but Prospero treats Ferdinand harshly. He secretly intends the two young people to marry, but first wants to test the sincerity of Ferdinand's love.

'You are three men of sin.' Ariel, in the form of a harpy, accuses Antonio, Alonso and Sebastian of their crimes against Prospero (centre, behind Ariel). The three are driven almost to madness by Ariel's enchantment and their own guilt.

Prospero agrees to the marriage of Miranda and Ferdinand. To celebrate the betrothal, he arranges a spectacular entertainment.

Caliban (centre), Stephano and Trinculo plot to kill Prospero and make Stephano king of the island. But Ariel overhears and reports this to Prospero. The plotters suffer all kinds of humiliation when they are brought to Prospero.

Prospero finally has all his enemies in his power, but learning
from Ariel (left) he decides that mercy is superior to revenge.
He forgives all those who have done him wrong.

Naples and Milan are united by the marriage of Miranda
and Ferdinand. Prospero sets Ariel free and bids farewell
to the audience as he prepares to return home to Milan.

List of characters

The island

PROSPERO the rightful Duke of Milan
MIRANDA his daughter
ARIEL an airy spirit
CALIBAN a savage and deformed slave
SPIRITS in Prospero's service
IRIS
CERES
JUNO } characters in the masque
NYMPHS
REAPERS

The shipwrecked royal court

ALONSO King of Naples
FERDINAND Alonso's son
SEBASTIAN Alonso's brother
ANTONIO Prospero's brother, the usurping Duke of Milan
GONZALO an honest old councillor
ADRIAN
FRANCISCO } lords
STEPHANO a drunken butler
TRINCULO a jester

The ship's crew

MASTER the captain
BOATSWAIN
MARINERS

The play takes place on a ship and an island

The Master commands the Boatswain to save the ship from running aground. The Boatswain gives instructions to the sailors but finds his work hampered by the courtiers. He orders them to go back to their cabins.

Stagecraft

Staging the storm (in large groups)

This opening scene is very dramatic: it takes place on a ship at sea during a terrible storm. How can the fury of the waves and wind be shown on stage? In some productions, the scene is played on a bare stage, without props or scenery – the illusion of a ship caught in a tempest is created only by lighting, sounds and the actors' movements. Other productions use an elaborate set to create a realistic ship.

a Begin a Director's Journal, in which you write down ideas relating to the play in performance. Try to think like a director, focusing on bringing the words to life. Add to your journal as you read the play.

b Consider how you would perform this opening scene. In your group, hold a discussion using the prompts below, then act out the scene. There are six individual speaking parts, and you can have as many sailors as you want.

- Explore ways of performing the first stage direction:
  'A *tempestuous noise of thunder and lightning heard*'.
- How can actors' movements suggest a ship caught in a storm?
- How might you convey the sense of fear and crisis? These are people who are desperately trying to save their lives: do they panic or are they well disciplined?
- What simple props might suggest a ship? One production had only a large ship's wheel at the back of the stage, and the sailors struggled to turn it to keep the ship on course. What would you use?

tempestuous very stormy and loud

Boatswain (pronounced 'bo-s'n') the man in charge of discipline on board a ship

What cheer? what news?

Good friend

mariners sailors

Fall to't yarely get a move on

Bestir quickly

Tend attend, listen

Blow … room enough you can blow as much as you like as long as we have space to sail in safety

Play the men act like men, command the sailors

keep below stay in your cabins

mar spoil, hinder

roarers wild waves and winds

whom (King Alonso)

Themes

Challenging authority (in pairs)

Throughout the play, traditional authority is challenged. The Boatswain is the character with the lowest social status in this scene, but it is he who takes charge. He orders the king and the other aristocrats off the deck.

- Do you think the Boatswain should defer to his social superiors, or is it important that he assumes control at this critical moment? Consider the possible consequences of the Boatswain's actions. Share your conclusions with other pairs.

The Tempest

Act 1 Scene 1
A ship at sea

A tempestuous noise of thunder and lightning heard. Enter a
SHIPMASTER, *a* BOATSWAIN *and* MARINERS

MASTER   Boatswain!

BOATSWAIN   Here, master. What cheer?

MASTER   Good; speak to th'mariners. Fall to't yarely, or we run our-
selves aground. Bestir, bestir!   *Exit*

BOATSWAIN   Heigh, my hearts! Cheerly, cheerly, my hearts! Yare, yare!   5
Take in the topsail. Tend to th'master's whistle. [*To the storm*] Blow
till thou burst thy wind, if room enough!

Enter ALONSO, SEBASTIAN, ANTONIO, FERDINAND,
GONZALO *and others*

ALONSO   Good boatswain, have care. Where's the master? Play the
men.

BOATSWAIN   I pray now, keep below.   10

ANTONIO   Where is the master, boatswain?

BOATSWAIN   Do you not hear him? You mar our labour – keep your
cabins. You do assist the storm.

GONZALO   Nay, good, be patient.

BOASTWAIN   When the sea is. Hence! What cares these roarers for the   15
name of king? To cabin. Silence! Trouble us not.

GONZALO   Good, yet remember whom thou hast aboard.

The Boatswain reminds Gonzalo of humanity's weakness in the face of nature's violence. Gonzalo finds comfort in the Boatswain's face. The Boatswain again rebukes the courtiers, and is cursed in return.

Themes

Humans and nature (whole class)

In the script opposite, the Boatswain raises another theme that recurs throughout the play – the relationship between humans and nature: 'if you can command these elements to silence … use your authority' (lines 19–20).

- Hold a class debate. One side argues that nature is humanity's opponent and must be controlled. The other side argues that nature is humanity's friend and should be respected.

1 'he hath no drowning mark upon him' (in pairs)

Gonzalo seems to 'read' the Boatswain's face, deciding that he is not destined to die by drowning, but rather by hanging. Is Gonzalo trusting to fate, being cynical, or trying to find humour in a desperate situation?

a How would you advise the actor playing Gonzalo to deliver these words? Try out different readings.

b Write down the ideas that are explored in lines 18–29, considering in particular the themes of fate and chance.

2 'the rope of his destiny'

This play is rich in **imagery** (see 'The language of *The Tempest*', pp. 164–5). In lines 25–9, Gonzalo uses complex imagery of a hangman's noose beginning to resemble an umbilical cord.

a Draw this image in a way that captures the richness of the language and the idea being expressed here.

b With others in your class, discuss what is lost and what is gained by turning these words into an image.

Characters

What does the language tell us? (in fours)

Look at the language used by the Boatswain and Gonzalo in the script opposite. Compare it to that used by Sebastian and Antonio.

- Discuss what each character's choice of words reveals about them and then act out lines 32–41. What are the dominant emotions expressed here? Anger? Fear? Acceptance? Denial? Think about the humour as well as the terror of the scene.

None … myself I am nearest to myself

councillor advisor

work … present stop the storm

hand a rope work (handle a rope)

mischance disaster

hap happen

Methinks I think

complexion face, appearance

cable three-twisted rope for an anchor

for our own … advantage our own anchor is of little help

Bring her … main-course use the mainsail

office captain's whistle

give o'er stop work

mind deliberate intention

whoreson son of a prostitute

I'll warrant … drowning I guarantee he won't drown

unstanched wench talkative or immoral woman

BOATSWAIN   None that I more love than myself. You are a councillor; if you can command these elements to silence, and work a peace of the present, we will not hand a rope more – use your authority. If   20
you cannot, give thanks you have lived so long, and make yourself ready in your cabin for the mischance of the hour, if it so hap. [*To the Mariners*] Cheerly, good hearts. [*To the courtiers*] Out of our way, I say.

[*Exeunt Boatswain with Mariners, followed by Alonso,*
Sebastian, Antonio, Ferdinand]

GONZALO   I have great comfort from this fellow. Methinks he hath no   25
drowning mark upon him, his complexion is perfect gallows. Stand fast, good Fate, to his hanging; make the rope of his destiny our cable, for our own doth little advantage. If he be not born to be hanged, our case is miserable.   *Exit*

Enter BOATSWAIN

BOATSWAIN   Down with the topmast! Yare, lower, lower! Bring her to   30
try with main-course.

A cry within

Enter SEBASTIAN, ANTONIO *and* GONZALO

A plague upon this howling! They are louder than the weather, or our office. [*To the lords*] Yet again? What do you here? Shall we give o'er and drown? Have you a mind to sink?

SEBASTIAN   A pox o'your throat, you bawling, blasphemous, in-   35
charitable dog.

BOATSWAIN   Work you then.

ANTONIO   Hang, cur, hang, you whoreson, insolent noisemaker, we are less afraid to be drowned than thou art.

GONZALO   I'll warrant him from drowning, though the ship were no   40
stronger than a nutshell, and as leaky as an unstanched wench.

The Boatswain orders action to save the ship, but disaster strikes. Antonio again curses the Boatswain. The crew abandon hope. Gonzalo accepts whatever is to come, but wishes for death on land.

1 'All lost ... all lost' (in small groups)

There is complete chaos on stage during the final part of this first scene. In what they believe are their final moments, all the characters behave in different ways. Some call on God's mercy in prayer. Others say farewell to each other. The Boatswain takes a drink (line 45).

- Each person takes a character from the script opposite. Prepare a tableau (a 'freeze-frame', like a photograph) of these final moments. Think carefully about the expression on each character's face – what emotions do you want to portray? Practise your tableau, then show it to the rest of the class.
- Take it in turns to break out of your tableau and describe – in your own words – how your character feels at this moment.

Write about it

The forces of fate

The fate of the sailors and their royal passengers seems to be decided. However, as we shall see, there are other forces at work that will decide whether they live or die.

- Read Scene I again, then write three paragraphs explaining how much control you think the characters have over their lives at this point. What forces are shaping their actions? Think about what most affects what they are doing and saying. Remember to refer to the script in your writing.

Lay her a-hold heave-to (furl the sail)

lay her off sail out to sea (the Boatswain changes his order)

must ... cold? let us have a warming drink (of alcohol)

merely utterly

wide-chopped big-mouthed

ten tides (pirates were condemned to be hanged and to have three tides wash over their bodies before being taken down; Antonio's comment is an exaggeration)

gape at wid'st to glut him open up to swallow him

a thousand furlongs (a furlong is about 200 metres)

long heath heather

brown furze gorse

The wills above God's will

fain rather

BOATSWAIN Lay her a-hold, a-hold; set her two courses. Off to sea
again; lay her off!

Enter MARINERS, *wet*

MARINERS All lost! To prayers, to prayers, all lost!

BOATSWAIN What, must our mouths be cold?   45

GONZALO The king and prince at prayers! Let's assist them,
For our case is as theirs.

SEBASTIAN   I'm out of patience.

ANTONIO We're merely cheated of our lives by drunkards.
This wide-chopped rascal – would thou mightst lie drowning
The washing of ten tides!

GONZALO   He'll be hanged yet,   50
Though every drop of water swear against it,
And gape at wid'st to glut him.

                              [*Exeunt Boatswain and Mariners*]
                    A confused noise within
                    Mercy on us!

[VOICES OFF STAGE] 'We split, we split!' – 'Farewell, my wife and children!' –
'Farewell, brother!' – 'We split, we split, we split!'

ANTONIO Let's all sink wi'th'king.

SEBASTIAN   Let's take leave of him.   55

                              [*Exeunt Sebastian and Antonio*]

GONZALO Now would I give a thousand furlongs of sea for an acre of
barren ground – long heath, brown furze, anything. The wills above
be done, but I would fain die a dry death.   *Exit*

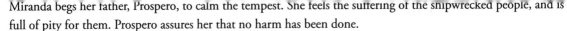

1 Visualising Prospero (in pairs)

We learn from Miranda's first speech that her father, Prospero, has the power to create storms and control the seas.

a How do you visualise Prospero? With a partner, talk about how he might appear.

b Look at the ways in which different productions have presented Prospero in the photographs throughout this book. Which one is closest to your own imagining of this character? How would you present him differently? Sketch your own ideas for Prospero's 'look'.

---

art magical powers

roar great noise

allay calm

The sky … fire out the sky seems filled with tar, which would become liquid and rain down as it is heated by the lightning but for the waves that rise up to extinguish the flames

welkin's cheek sky's face

brave noble, fine

creature human being

or ere before

fraughting souls terrified passengers

Be collected be calm

amazement wonder

Language in the play

Conjuring the storm (in fours)

Miranda's first speech (lines 1–13) is a vivid description of the storm as it is happening.

a Take it in turns to read the speech aloud, changing speaker at each punctuation mark. Emphasise the imagery she uses to describe the storm.

b Talk together about Miranda's 'storm' imagery. How does it create atmosphere for the audience? Make some notes and then share your thoughts with other groups.

c What does Miranda's language in the script opposite tell us about her character? Draw up a list of adjectives you would use to describe her.

2 'no harm done'? (in pairs)

a Look at the exchange between Prospero and Miranda in lines 13–21. Shakespeare uses **anaphora** – the repetition of words in successive clauses (see p. 167) – in Prospero's words 'No harm'. It is as though he is trying to reassure his daughter that he is benevolent. But what do you think are his motives? Discuss this in your pairs.

b What are your first impressions of Prospero and Miranda, and of their relationship? By yourself, write down your thoughts, then swap these notes with your partner. How are your impressions similar? How do they differ?

Act 1 Scene 2
The island

Enter PROSPERO *and* MIRANDA

MIRANDA	If by your art, my dearest father, you have
	Put the wild waters in this roar, allay them.
	The sky it seems would pour down stinking pitch,
	But that the sea, mounting to th'welkin's cheek,
	Dashes the fire out. O, I have suffered
	With those that I saw suffer! A brave vessel,
	Who had no doubt some noble creature in her,
	Dashed all to pieces. O, the cry did knock
	Against my very heart! Poor souls, they perished.
	Had I been any god of power, I would
	Have sunk the sea within the earth, or ere
	It should the good ship so have swallowed, and
	The fraughting souls within her.
PROSPERO	Be collected;
	No more amazement. Tell your piteous heart
	There's no harm done.
MIRANDA	O, woe the day.
PROSPERO	No harm.
	I have done nothing but in care of thee –
	Of thee my dear one, thee my daughter – who
	Art ignorant of what thou art, nought knowing
	Of whence I am, nor that I am more better
	Than Prospero, master of a full poor cell,
	And thy no greater father.
MIRANDA	More to know
	Did never meddle with my thoughts.

5

10

15

20

Prospero decides to tell Miranda her life story. He again assures her that no one was hurt in the shipwreck. He questions her about what she remembers, then reveals that he was once duke of Milan.

1 Prospero's 'magic garment'

Prospero wears a 'magic garment', which gives him the supernatural powers that he calls his 'art'. In stage productions, this garment is often a cloak, richly decorated with magical symbols.

- Design your own version of Prospero's 'magic garment', using symbols to suggest particular powers.

Language in the play

'In the dark backward and abysm of time' (in pairs)

Line 50 is a good example of the rich imagery in *The Tempest*. Instead of saying 'long ago' or 'in the dim and distant past', Prospero says 'In the dark backward and abysm of time'.

- Try translating this line into modern English prose, then discuss your different versions. What has been lost from the original in your modern version?

2 'A prince of power'

Over the course of lines 53–88, we discover many things about Prospero and Miranda.

- After you have read this important exchange, write a short account (between one and three paragraphs) that explains their change of fortunes and their link with the passengers on the sunken ship.

Characters

Prospero's story: a first impression (in pairs)

In lines 53–186, Prospero tells the story of how he and Miranda came to the island.

a Take parts and read the first part of this story (lines 53–88). Don't worry about words and phrases you may not understand. Just treat the read-through as a way of gaining a first impression of Prospero's overthrow and his journey to the island.

b Read through this part of the script again, taking turns in role as Prospero and as a voice coach, offering advice. What suggestions would you make about pitch, pace, pause and accompanying gestures to best portray Prospero's character and emotions?

direful spectacle terrible sight
very virtue essence
provision foresight
soul person
perdition loss
Betid happened

bootless inquisition unsuccessful enquiry

Out … old over three years old

Of any thing … remembrance describe to me any memories that you recall

And … warrants it's more like a dream than a clear memory

tended waited on

aught ere anything before
thou mayst you might remember

PROSPERO   'Tis time
I should inform thee farther. Lend thy hand
And pluck my magic garment from me – so –
     [*Miranda assists Prospero; his cloak is laid aside*]
Lie there my art. Wipe thou thine eyes; have comfort.   25
The direful spectacle of the wrack which touched
The very virtue of compassion in thee,
I have with such provision in mine art
So safely ordered, that there is no soul,
No, not so much perdition as an hair   30
Betid to any creature in the vessel
Which thou heard'st cry, which thou saw'st sink. Sit down,
For thou must now know farther.
                    [*Miranda sits*]
MIRANDA   You have often
Begun to tell me what I am, but stopped
And left me to a bootless inquisition,   35
Concluding, 'Stay: not yet.'
PROSPERO   The hour's now come;
The very minute bids thee ope thine ear,
Obey, and be attentive. Canst thou remember
A time before we came unto this cell?
I do not think thou canst, for then thou wast not   40
Out three years old.
MIRANDA   Certainly, sir, I can.
PROSPERO By what? By any other house, or person?
Of any thing the image, tell me, that
Hath kept with thy remembrance.
MIRANDA   'Tis far off;
And rather like a dream, than an assurance   45
That my remembrance warrants. Had I not
Four or five women once, that tended me?
PROSPERO Thou hadst, and more, Miranda. But how is't
That this lives in thy mind? What seest thou else
In the dark backward and abysm of time?   50
If thou rememb'rest aught ere thou cam'st here,
How thou cam'st here thou mayst.
MIRANDA   But that I do not.
PROSPERO Twelve year since, Miranda, twelve year since,
Thy father was the Duke of Milan and
A prince of power –

Prospero again confirms that he was once the duke of Milan. As Prospero wanted to pursue his studies, he made his brother, Antonio, ruler of the state. The treacherous Antonio seized all power from Prospero.

Stagecraft

Prospero and Antonio: brothers and enemies (in fours)

Prospero describes how he was once the unchallenged ruler of Milan, the most important state in Italy: 'Through all the signories it was the first, / And Prospero the prime duke.' However, because of his overwhelming interest in acquiring magical skills, he entrusted the government of Milan to Antonio, his brother. This was a mistake – Antonio usurped him and took control of Milan.

a Split into two pairs. One pair takes the parts of Prospero and Miranda and reads lines 66–87 aloud. As they speak, the other pair mimes the actions described. Afterwards, swap roles and repeat the activity. As you read, think about the range of emotions Prospero is feeling. (Consider how the language is disjointed, suggesting anger.)

b In the Director's Journal that you began on page 2, write down how you would want the depict the relationship between these characters during this scene.

Characters

Miranda: disrespectful or distracted?

Miranda's language gives the impression that she is a dutiful daughter. However, she also appears to be rather distracted as Prospero recounts his story.

a Why do you think this is? What might she be thinking about? What tasks might she be doing around their home as Prospero tells his tale?

b Write notes to the actor playing Miranda, explaining how you think she should perform these lines.

1 'rapt in secret studies'

Consider Prospero's story from Antonio's perspective. He could argue that the duke had become too caught up in his magical studies, and that he was failing in his duties to the people of Milan.

• As you read Prospero's story, write down any ideas you have that might support Antonio's actions. Think about why Shakespeare may have wanted his audience to consider both sides of the situation.

piece of virtue model of faithfulness

no worse issued similarly noble

heaved thence thrown out of Milan

holp hither helped here

o'th'teen of the trouble

is ... remembrance I've forgotten

perfidious treacherous

put ... my state gave rule over my dukedom

signories Italian states

prime highest ranking

transported / And rapt in enchanted by

secret studies magical skills

heedfully attentively

Being ... pèrfected once he had mastered politics

grant suits bestow favours

who ... over-topping who to stop for being overly ambitious

The creatures that were mine those who owed their positions to me

changed 'em ... formed 'em changed the support of officials and created new honours to gain new supporters

the key ... office the means of controlling political office

verdure sap, life

MIRANDA	Sir, are not you my father?	55
PROSPERO	Thy mother was a piece of virtue, and	
	She said thou wast my daughter; and thy father	
	Was Duke of Milan; and his only heir,	
	And princess, no worse issued.	
MIRANDA	O the heavens!	
	What foul play had we, that we came from thence?	60
	Or blessèd was't we did?	
PROSPERO	Both, both, my girl.	
	By foul play, as thou say'st, were we heaved thence,	
	But blessedly holp hither.	
MIRANDA	O, my heart bleeds	
	To think o'th'teen that I have turned you to,	
	Which is from my remembrance. Please you, farther.	65
PROSPERO	My brother and thy uncle, called Antonio –	
	I pray thee mark me, that a brother should	
	Be so perfidious – he, whom next thyself	
	Of all the world I loved, and to him put	
	The manage of my state, as at that time	70
	Through all the signories it was the first,	
	And Prospero the prime duke, being so reputed	
	In dignity, and for the liberal arts	
	Without a parallel; those being all my study,	
	The government I cast upon my brother,	75
	And to my state grew stranger, being transported	
	And rapt in secret studies. Thy false uncle –	
	Dost thou attend me? –	
MIRANDA	Sir, most heedfully.	
PROSPERO	Being once pèrfected how to grant suits,	
	How to deny them; who t'advance, and who	80
	To trash for over-topping; new created	
	The creatures that were mine, I say, or changed 'em,	
	Or else new formed 'em; having both the key	
	Of officer, and office, set all hearts i'th'state	
	To what tune pleased his ear, that now he was	85
	The ivy which had hid my princely trunk,	
	And sucked my verdure out on't – thou attend'st not!	
MIRANDA	O good sir, I do.	

Prospero describes how his neglect of his duties aroused his brother's evil nature. Enjoying the benefits of playing the duke, Antonio aspired to the position himself, and plotted with Alonso, the king of Naples.

Language in the play
Antonio's ambition grows (in small groups)

Prospero passionately recalls his brother's treachery. Lines 88–116 show his angry state of mind. Match statements **a** to **k** below with the appropriate lines from the script opposite.

a I neglected the business of government.

b I sought privacy in order to study.

c But what I studied was beyond the citizens' interest or understanding.

d My retirement was the cause of my brother's evil acts.

e My absolute trust in him was completely betrayed.

f He abused my wealth and overtaxed my people,

g He came to believe his own lies that he was the duke.

h Therefore his ambition grew.

i He wished to become the part he played – the duke.

j I was content with my books. He took this as a sign that I was unfit to govern.

k Eager for power, he agreed to make Milan, hitherto independent, subordinate to the king of Naples.

Stagecraft
Prospero's growing anger

Miranda's line 106 ('Your tale, sir, would cure deafness') reveals just how worked up Prospero is becoming.

- In your Director's Journal, write out how you would stage this part of the scene. Have fun exploring Miranda as a long-suffering daughter and Prospero as an increasingly angry father. Think about where you would place the characters on the stage as these lines are spoken.

1 'Good wombs have borne bad sons'

In line 120, Miranda suggests that nature is not the sole determiner of character, but that we are also affected by our surroundings.

- From what you have read so far, write down five points that support Miranda's view, and five points that contradict it. Use quotations from the script to back up your points.

closeness secrecy

but … rate because I became withdrawn, I overestimated the value of my studies to others

beget bring out

sans bound without limit

thus lorded so like a duke

revènue wealth

into truth invented reality

of it of the lie

To credit to believe

o'th'substitution as a result of me giving up my position to him

executing … royalty the use of his apparent royal power

prerogative authority

Absolute Milan the real duke of Milan

temporal royalties worldly power

confederates makes a treaty with

So dry he was for sway so eager for power

tribute protection money

yet unbowed independent till now

condition treaty terms

event outcome

PROSPERO	I pray thee mark me:	
	I, thus neglecting worldly ends, all dedicated	
	To closeness, and the bettering of my mind	90
	With that which, but by being so retired,	
	O'er-prized all popular rate, in my false brother	
	Awaked an evil nature; and my trust,	
	Like a good parent, did beget of him	
	A falsehood, in its contrary as great	95
	As my trust was – which had indeed no limit,	
	A confidence sans bound. He being thus lorded,	
	Not only with what my revènue yielded,	
	But what my power might else exact – like one	
	Who, having into truth by telling of it,	100
	Made such a sinner of his memory	
	To credit his own lie – he did believe	
	He was indeed the duke, out o'th'substitution	
	And executing th'outward face of royalty	
	With all prerogative. Hence his ambition growing –	105
	Dost thou hear?	
MIRANDA	Your tale, sir, would cure deafness.	
PROSPERO	To have no screen between this part he played,	
	And him he played it for, he needs will be	
	Absolute Milan. Me, poor man, my library	
	Was dukedom large enough. Of temporal royalties	110
	He thinks me now incapable; confederates –	
	So dry he was for sway – wi'th'King of Naples	
	To give him annual tribute, do him homage,	
	Subject his coronet to his crown, and bend	
	The dukedom yet unbowed – alas, poor Milan –	115
	To most ignoble stooping.	
MIRANDA	O the heavens!	
PROSPERO	Mark his condition, and th'event, then tell me	
	If this might be a brother.	
MIRANDA	I should sin	
	To think but nobly of my grandmother –	
	Good wombs have borne bad sons.	

Alonso made a treaty with Antonio to overthrow Prospero. Antonio treacherously admitted Alonso's army into Milan. Prospero and Miranda were captured and cast adrift in a tiny, unseaworthy boat.

Stagecraft

Overthrowing Prospero (in small groups)

Prospero continues to tell his story. His old enemy, Alonso, king of Naples, agreed a treaty ('condition') with Antonio. The agreement was that, in exchange for ('in lieu o'th'premises') making Milan subordinate to Naples and for protection money ('tribute'), Alonso would overthrow Prospero and make Antonio duke of Milan. Under cover of darkness, the treacherous Antonio opened the city gates to give Alonso's accomplices ('ministers') the opportunity to capture Prospero and Miranda. The conspirators dared not kill Prospero because of his popularity. Instead, they abandoned him and his infant daughter in a tiny, unseaworthy boat ('A rotten carcass of a butt').

The script opposite is only part of Prospero's story, but it has great potential for drama. Try one or more of the following activities.

a **What if?** The influential Russian theatre director Stanislavski felt that the question 'What if?' was one of the most powerful tools for understanding a script. How many 'What ifs' can you ask of the speeches in the script opposite? For example, what if Prospero is exaggerating? How would we know? What if Miranda is becoming increasingly bored by the story? How would this affect the way the actors perform the scene? Split into pairs, with one of you asking 'What if …?' and the other answering the question. Afterwards, compare your ideas with other pairs in your group.

b **Notes for the actors** Each member of the group takes a speech (or part of a speech) from Prospero's story and writes detailed notes on how the two actors should speak and move. Then put your combined advice into action and perform the whole thing using your various notes.

c **Speak the lines** Experiment with ways of relating Prospero's story. For example, you could read his speeches rapidly, with the words tumbling out passionately as the former duke angrily recalls what happened. Alternatively, you could read the lines very slowly and reflectively, as if the experience was like a dream from long ago. Which style has the most dramatic impact?

inveterate of long standing

hearkens … suit listens to Antonio's proposal

in lieu o'th'premises receives Antonio's offer favourably

presently extirpate immediately expel (or destroy)

levied gathered

Fated destined

ministers servants and agents

hint occasion, event

wrings forces

impertinent irrelevant

wench daughter, loved one

durst not dared not

In few briefly

barque small boat

leagues sea miles

carcass skeleton

butt tub

hoist transferred

PROSPERO   Now the condition.   120
This King of Naples, being an enemy
To me inveterate, hearkens my brother's suit,
Which was, that he, in lieu o'th'premises
Of homage, and I know not how much tribute,
Should presently extirpate me and mine   125
Out of the dukedom, and confer fair Milan,
With all the honours, on my brother. Whereon,
A treacherous army levied, one midnight
Fated to th'purpose did Antonio open
The gates of Milan, and i'th'dead of darkness   130
The ministers for th'purpose hurried thence
Me, and thy crying self.

MIRANDA   Alack, for pity!
I, not remembering how I cried out then,
Will cry it o'er again; it is a hint
That wrings mine eyes to't.

PROSPERO   Hear a little further,   135
And then I'll bring thee to the present business
Which now's upon's; without the which, this story
Were most impertinent.

MIRANDA   Wherefore did they not
That hour destroy us?

PROSPERO   Well demanded, wench;
My tale provokes that question. Dear, they durst not,   140
So dear the love my people bore me; nor set
A mark so bloody on the business; but
With colours fairer painted their foul ends.
In few, they hurried us aboard a barque,
Bore us some leagues to sea, where they prepared   145
A rotten carcass of a butt, not rigged,
Nor tackle, sail, nor mast – the very rats
Instinctively have quit it. There they hoist us
To cry to th'sea, that roared to us; to sigh
To th'winds, whose pity sighing back again   150
Did us but loving wrong.

MIRANDA   Alack, what trouble
Was I then to you!

Prospero says that he found comfort and strength in Miranda's smile, in divine providence and in Gonzalo's help. He believes that Fortune now favours him, as his enemies are within his reach. He causes Miranda to fall asleep.

1 'Knowing I loved my books'

Gonzalo made sure that books were placed in the boat that carried Prospero unwillingly to exile.

a If you had to choose five possessions to take with you to a desert island, what would they be? They must be portable and either useful or of personal value (or both). If appropriate, bring them in to class and discuss why you have chosen them.

b Now think about Prospero. What does the fact that his most cherished objects are his books tell us about him and the society in which he lived? Share your ideas in groups or as a whole-class discussion.

Write about it

Duke and princess … father and daughter … exiles

The relationship between Prospero and Miranda is a complex one, and it raises a number of key themes that run through the play, including family, duty, status and exile.

* Reflect on these and other ideas in relation to the relationship described in this scene. Write either a 100-word summary of the story told by Prospero or an analysis of the representation of the father–daughter relationship in the first 186 lines of this scene.

cherubin guardian angel

Infusèd with a fortitude full of endurance
decked covered, ornamented

undergoing stomach the courage to go on

design plan
stuffs materials
steaded much greatly helped us

profit benefit

prescience foreknowledge, insight
zenith highest point of fortune
auspicious favourable
influence astrological power
court befriend, use
omit neglect
good dullness pleasant, timely sleepiness
give it way give in to it

PROSPERO	[*Sitting*] O, a cherubin
	Thou wast that did preserve me. Thou didst smile,
	Infusèd with a fortitude from heaven,
	When I have decked the sea with drops full salt,
	Under my burden groaned; which raised in me
	An undergoing stomach, to bear up
	Against what should ensue.
MIRANDA	How came we ashore?
PROSPERO	By providence divine.
	Some food we had, and some fresh water, that
	A noble Neapolitan, Gonzalo,
	Out of his charity – who being then appointed
	Master of this design – did give us, with
	Rich garments, linens, stuffs, and necessaries
	Which since have steaded much. So, of his gentleness,
	Knowing I loved my books, he furnished me
	From mine own library, with volumes that
	I prize above my dukedom.
MIRANDA	Would I might
	But ever see that man.
PROSPERO	[*Standing*] Now I arise,
	Sit still, and hear the last of our sea-sorrow.
	Here in this island we arrived, and here
	Have I, thy schoolmaster, made thee more profit
	Than other princes can, that have more time
	For vainer hours, and tutors not so careful.
MIRANDA	Heavens thank you for't. And now I pray you, sir –
	For still 'tis beating in my mind – your reason
	For raising this sea-storm?
PROSPERO	Know thus forth:
	By accident most strange, bountiful Fortune,
	Now my dear lady, hath mine enemies
	Brought to this shore; and by my prescience
	I find my zenith doth depend upon
	A most auspicious star, whose influence
	If now I court not, but omit, my fortunes
	Will ever after droop. Here cease more questions.
	Thou art inclined to sleep. 'Tis a good dullness,
	And give it way; I know thou canst not choose.

Line numbers: 155, 160, 165, 170, 175, 180, 185

Prospero calls Ariel, who reports that he has carried out Prospero's commands in exact detail. Ariel's miraculous display of fire caused terror on the ship. Ferdinand was the first passenger to leap overboard.

Stagecraft
The casting of Ariel

Ariel can be played by either a man or a woman. What sort of Ariel would you want in your production? How would you cast the part?

a In your Director's Journal, list the famous actors you think would be good for the part. Give brief reasons for each choice.

b Think about the relationship you would want to establish early on between Prospero ('great master') and his servant ('brave spirit'). Share your thoughts with a partner. Are your ideas similar?

1 Act Ariel's story of the shipwreck

Lines 187–215 offer exciting opportunities for acting.

a **Whole class** Everyone learns a very short section of Ariel's lines from the script opposite. One person plays Prospero, and stands in the centre of the room. In turn, each Ariel runs to join Prospero, speaking 'his' words and making appropriate gestures. The person who has the words 'more momentary / And sight-outrunning were not' has a challenging task: how can you outrun sight?

b **In pairs** Choose a short section for one of you to read out while the other echoes it. Try different styles of echoing, such as whispering, questioning, and speaking emphatically, slowly and rapidly. Discuss which is the more effective and why you think that is.

c **On your own** Read Ariel's lines aloud while walking around. Change direction abruptly at each punctuation mark, and add suitable gestures.

Themes
The use (and abuse) of power (in fours)

Ferdinand's actions convey something of the atmosphere on board the ship. Ariel's description of the chaos can be portrayed in different ways. Some productions emphasise its mischievousness; others depict it as something more terrifying.

- Discuss whether you think Prospero is right to take revenge on Antonio and all his crew. Two of you defend Prospero and two criticise him. Share your ideas with other groups and agree on the top five points made for and against Prospero's actions.

---

grave sir most wise master

task command
all his quality all his fellow spirits
to point in exact detail

beak prow
in the waist in the middle of the boat
flamed amazement appeared as a frightening fire
yards poles supporting the sails
bowsprit pole on which the foremast is secured
distinctly separately
Jove Jupiter (king of the gods)
precursors forerunners
momentary short lived
sight-outrunning quicker than they could follow with their eyes
Neptune god of the sea
coil turmoil, confusion
fever of the mad fever that those who are insane might feel
tricks of desperation despairing actions

hair up-staring hair standing on end

nigh shore near land

[Miranda sleeps]
Come away, servant, come; I'm ready now.
Approach, my Ariel. Come!

Enter ARIEL

ARIEL   All hail, great master, grave sir, hail! I come
            To answer thy best pleasure; be't to fly,   190
            To swim, to dive into the fire, to ride
            On the curled clouds. To thy strong bidding task
            Ariel, and all his quality.

PROSPERO   Hast thou, spirit, performed to point the tempest
            That I bade thee?

ARIEL   To every article.   195
            I boarded the king's ship. Now on the beak,
            Now in the waist, the deck, in every cabin,
            I flamed amazement. Sometime I'd divide
            And burn in many places; on the topmast,
            The yards and bowsprit, would I flame distinctly,   200
            Then meet and join. Jove's lightning, the precursors
            O'th'dreadful thunder-claps, more momentary
            And sight-outrunning were not; the fire and cracks
            Of sulphurous roaring the most mighty Neptune
            Seem to besiege, and make his bold waves tremble,   205
            Yea, his dread trident shake.

PROSPERO   My brave spirit!
            Who was so firm, so constant, that this coil
            Would not infect his reason?

ARIEL   Not a soul
            But felt a fever of the mad, and played
            Some tricks of desperation. All but mariners   210
            Plunged in the foaming brine and quit the vessel,
            Then all a-fire with me; the king's son Ferdinand,
            With hair up-staring – then like reeds, not hair –
            Was the first man that leaped; cried 'Hell is empty,
            And all the devils are here.'

PROSPERO   Why that's my spirit.   215
            But was not this nigh shore?

ARIEL   Close by, my master.

PROSPERO   But are they, Ariel, safe?

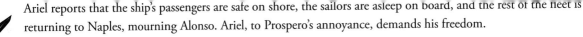

Write about it

Making sense of the storm (in pairs)

Ariel explains that the other boats in the fleet are returning safely home, but that they have witnessed the destruction of the king's ship.

- One of you steps into role as a sailor in the fleet heading home. Write to a member of your family describing the events that have taken place. You can write your letter in Shakespearean prose or in modern English.
- The other person takes on the role of a crew member who is now safe and 'dispersed … 'bout the isle'. Write his diary entry. How would he make sense of what has happened (look carefully at lines 217–19)? You can write in modern or Shakespearean prose, but whichever style you choose, you should try to convey the information using rich and evocative language.

sustaining buoyant (supporting in the sea)

troops groups

odd angle remote corner
His arms … knot his arms folded in a melancholy way

deep nook secret bay

still-vexed always stormy
under hatches below deck
charm spell
suffered labour exhaustion

float sea

1 Ariel: a resentful servant?

In traditional tales, the spirits who serve magicians are often resentful and the magicians are never completely in control. Prospero and Ariel seem to be no exception. How does Ariel make his demand for freedom: resentfully, politely or in some other way?
How does Prospero reply?

charge duty

- Advise the actors on how to deliver lines 240–50. You may find it useful to think about which sentences are interrogative (questions) or declarative (statements).

mid-season noon
two glasses two o'clock
'twixt six and now between now (2 p.m.) and 6 p.m. (four hours)
most preciously without waste
give me pains demand more work from me

before the time be out before your agreed period of service is over
prithee pray you

bate me let me off

ARIEL	Not a hair perished;
	On their sustaining garments not a blemish,
	But fresher than before. And as thou bad'st me,
	In troops I have dispersed them 'bout the isle.	220
	The king's son have I landed by himself,
	Whom I left cooling of the air with sighs
	In an odd angle of the isle, and sitting,
	His arms in this sad knot.
PROSPERO	Of the king's ship,
	The mariners, say how thou hast disposed,	225
	And all the rest o'th'fleet?
ARIEL	Safely in harbour
	Is the king's ship, in the deep nook, where once
	Thou call'dst me up at midnight to fetch dew
	From the still-vexed Bermudas, there she's hid;
	The mariners all under hatches stowed,	230
	Who, with a charm joined to their suffered labour,
	I've left asleep. And for the rest o'th'fleet –
	Which I dispersed – they all have met again,
	And are upon the Mediterranean float
	Bound sadly home for Naples,	235
	Supposing that they saw the king's ship wracked,
	And his great person perish.
PROSPERO	Ariel, thy charge
	Exactly is performed; but there's more work.
	What is the time o'th'day?
ARIEL	Past the mid-season.
PROSPERO	At least two glasses. The time 'twixt six and now	240
	Must by us both be spent most preciously.
ARIEL	Is there more toil? Since thou dost give me pains,
	Let me remember thee what thou hast promised,
	Which is not yet performed me.
PROSPERO	How now? Moody?
	What is't thou canst demand?
ARIEL	My liberty.	245
PROSPERO	Before the time be out? No more.
ARIEL	I prithee,
	Remember I have done thee worthy service,
	Told thee no lies, made no mistakings, served
	Without or grudge or grumblings. Thou did promise
	To bate me a full year.

Prospero rebukes Ariel, accusing him of resentfulness. Prospero reminds Ariel of Sycorax who, enraged by Ariel's refusal to obey her, imprisoned him inside a tree, where he suffered agony for twelve years.

1 What is your image of Ariel? (in pairs)

Ariel is Prospero's servant. His past errands have taken him to the ocean floor, to the freezing north wind, and to rivers running deep underground (lines 252–6).

- Look at the photographs of actors portraying Ariel on pages v, vii, x, 22, 26, 98, 103, 172 and 179. Which comes closest to your own image of an Ariel who could perform such amazing feats?

Language in the play
Ariel – from captivity to freedom

Lines 252–6 contrast with lines 274–80 in describing Ariel's experiences serving Prospero and enduring imprisonment by the witch Sycorax.

- Write a paragraph describing the visual imagery conjured by Prospero's language in these two passages. What does this imagery reveal about his character?

2 'The foul witch Sycorax' (in small groups)

No one really knows why Shakespeare decided to use the name Sycorax for the witch who tormented Ariel. Perhaps the name comes from two Greek words: *sys* (sow) and *korax* (raven). Whatever Sycorax's name means, we know she 'with age and envy / Was grown into a hoop'. This physical deformity was meant to indicate her moral deformity and evil nature.

- Compile a list of all references to witchcraft and evil as they relate to Sycorax in the script opposite.

Write about it
Diary of a citizen of Algiers

We are told that despite her 'mischiefs manifold' and 'sorceries terrible', Sycorax was not killed by the citizens of Algiers: 'For one thing she did / They would not take her life'. What was the amazing 'one thing' she did that so impressed (or frightened) the citizens that they spared her life?

- Imagine Sycorax's life story and write the diary of someone who observed her closely when she lived in Algiers, attracting the attention of the citizens through her 'mischiefs manifold'.

---

think'st it much resent having

do me business work for me

grown ... hoop became hunched over and deformed

blue-eyed sky-coloured or bleary (eyes here could refer to the eyelids and the area round the eye)

with child pregnant

delicate fine, exquisite in nature

abhorred hateful

grand hests terrible commands

potent ministers powerful spirits

unmitigable resistant to any attempt to calm down

cloven split

rift cleft

vent emit

as mill-wheels strike constantly, as the paddles of a mill-wheel strike the water

litter give birth to

whelp dog

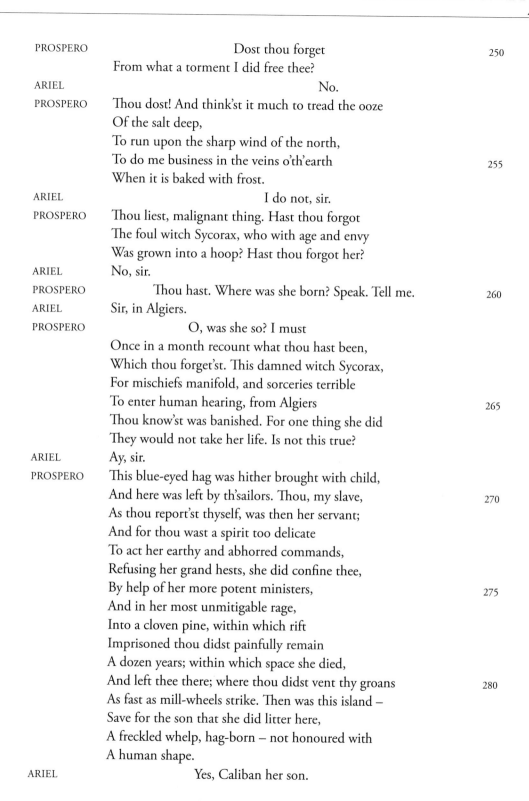

PROSPERO	Dost thou forget	250
	From what a torment I did free thee?	
ARIEL	No.	
PROSPERO	Thou dost! And think'st it much to tread the ooze	
	Of the salt deep,	
	To run upon the sharp wind of the north,	
	To do me business in the veins o'th'earth	255
	When it is baked with frost.	
ARIEL	I do not, sir.	
PROSPERO	Thou liest, malignant thing. Hast thou forgot	
	The foul witch Sycorax, who with age and envy	
	Was grown into a hoop? Hast thou forgot her?	
ARIEL	No, sir.	
PROSPERO	Thou hast. Where was she born? Speak. Tell me.	260
ARIEL	Sir, in Algiers.	
PROSPERO	O, was she so? I must	
	Once in a month recount what thou hast been,	
	Which thou forget'st. This damned witch Sycorax,	
	For mischiefs manifold, and sorceries terrible	
	To enter human hearing, from Algiers	265
	Thou know'st was banished. For one thing she did	
	They would not take her life. Is not this true?	
ARIEL	Ay, sir.	
PROSPERO	This blue-eyed hag was hither brought with child,	
	And here was left by th'sailors. Thou, my slave,	270
	As thou report'st thyself, was then her servant;	
	And for thou wast a spirit too delicate	
	To act her earthy and abhorred commands,	
	Refusing her grand hests, she did confine thee,	
	By help of her more potent ministers,	275
	And in her most unmitigable rage,	
	Into a cloven pine, within which rift	
	Imprisoned thou didst painfully remain	
	A dozen years; within which space she died,	
	And left thee there; where thou didst vent thy groans	280
	As fast as mill-wheels strike. Then was this island –	
	Save for the son that she did litter here,	
	A freckled whelp, hag-born – not honoured with	
	A human shape.	
ARIEL	Yes, Caliban her son.	

Prospero describes how he released Ariel, but threatens further punishment if Ariel continues to complain. He orders Ariel to disguise himself as an invisible sea-nymph, wakes Miranda and proposes to visit Caliban.

1 Imprisonment and release (in small groups)

Lines 286–93 vividly describe Ariel's torment as he was imprisoned in the 'cloven pine' (a split pine tree), and his subsequent release by Prospero.

a Read this section, then discuss how Prospero's violent imagery creates dramatic effect at this point in the play.

b In groups, create a tableau representing Ariel's imprisonment. Try to include the 'unmitigable rage' of Sycorax, the suffering of Ariel and the magic art of Prospero that set the spirit free.

2 Prospero and Ariel: master and servant (in pairs)

Read lines 290–305. Prospero reminds Ariel of his imprisonment on the island before his master's arrival. Reminded of how much he owes Prospero, Ariel promises not to be moody or keep demanding his liberty.

- Experiment with ways of reading these lines. What tone of voice should each character use? Does Ariel ask for pardon humbly and sincerely, or is he resentful? Is Prospero more like an indulgent teacher, an angry parent, a hard taskmaster or something else?

Stagecraft

Ariel's invisible shape

In lines 302–5, Prospero tells Ariel to make himself invisible to everyone except him.

- How would you ensure that the audience (and Prospero) can see Ariel, but no one else on stage knows he is there? Write your ideas in your Director's Journal.

penetrate the breasts evoke pity

made gape opened up

murmur'st rebelliously complain
rend split

correspondent responsive, answerable

discharge thee relieve you of your duties

diligence care

Heaviness drowsiness

villain both evil and low-born

miss do without
offices tasks
profit benefit
earth (emphasising Caliban's elemental opposition to the airy Ariel)

PROSPERO	Dull thing, I say so: he, that Caliban	285
	Whom now I keep in service. Thou best know'st	
	What torment I did find thee in. Thy groans	
	Did make wolves howl, and penetrate the breasts	
	Of ever-angry bears. It was a torment	
	To lay upon the damned, which Sycorax	290
	Could not again undo. It was mine art,	
	When I arrived and heard thee, that made gape	
	The pine, and let thee out.	
ARIEL	I thank thee, master.	
PROSPERO	If thou more murmur'st, I will rend an oak	
	And peg thee in his knotty entrails till	295
	Thou hast howled away twelve winters.	
ARIEL	Pardon, master.	
	I will be correspondent to command	
	And do my spiriting gently.	
PROSPERO	Do so;	
	And after two days I will discharge thee.	
ARIEL	That's my noble master! What shall I do?	300
	Say what? What shall I do?	
PROSPERO	Go make thyself	
	Like to a nymph o'th'sea. Be subject to	
	No sight but thine and mine, invisible	
	To every eye-ball else. Go take this shape	
	And hither come in't. Go! Hence with diligence.	305

Exit [*Ariel*]

[*To Miranda*] Awake, dear heart, awake; thou hast slept well,
Awake.

MIRANDA	The strangeness of your story put	
	Heaviness in me.	
PROSPERO	Shake it off. Come on,	
	We'll visit Caliban, my slave, who never	
	Yields us kind answer.	
MIRANDA	'Tis a villain, sir,	310
	I do not love to look on.	
PROSPERO	But as 'tis	
	We cannot miss him. He does make our fire,	
	Fetch in our wood, and serves in offices	
	That profit us. What ho! Slave! Caliban!	
	Thou earth, thou! Speak!	

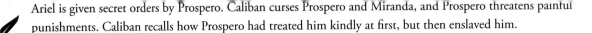

Stagecraft

'*Enter* CALIBAN'

Prospero shouts for Caliban with insults. He calls him his slave – a word he never uses to describe Ariel. Although Caliban answers him rudely from off stage, his entrance is delayed.

- How would you stage this entrance when it eventually occurs? What is going on both off stage and on stage while Prospero waits for Caliban? How does he look and act when he finally appears? Notice that 'Caliban' is almost an anagram of 'cannibal' – does this affect how you imagine him to look and behave?
- Make notes in your Director's Journal, describing how you would stage this part of the scene in a modern performance.

1 'This island's mine' (in pairs)

Who has the right to own the island? Many people believe that Caliban's experience is typical of what happens to any race subjected to colonisation (see 'Perspectives and themes', pp. 154–5). When Prospero came to the island, he treated Caliban kindly, but then made him his slave.

- Explore the story that unfolds in lines 332–62 from the point of view of both Caliban and Prospero. Take parts as one of these two characters and argue for your own claim over the island. Use quotations from the play to support your case.

Language in the play

Punctuation

Think about how Caliban's language makes you feel as you read lines 331–45 while walking round the classroom. As you walk, change direction on each punctuation mark, using the following rules:

- At each full stop, make a full about-turn (180 degrees).
- At each comma, semi-colon and dash, make a half turn (90 degrees to your right or left).
- Think of a gesture to make at every exclamation mark (such as stamping your foot or clicking your fingers).

Which words or lines stood out for you during this activity? How did it change your understanding of Caliban's emotions and his feelings towards Prospero?

Fine apparition well disguised
quaint clever, elegant

got fathered
dam mother

raven bird of ill-omen, particularly associated with witchcraft
fen marsh, bog
south-west unhealthy wind

urchins hedgehogs, goblins
vast of night long stretch of night
pinched … honeycomb the marks of the pinches will be as numerous as the cells in a honeycomb

bigger light … less sun and moon

qualities special places
brine-pits salt pits
charms spells

sty me imprison me like a pig

CALIBAN	(*Within*) There's wood enough within.	315
PROSPERO	Come forth, I say; there's other business for thee.	
	Come, thou tortoise, when?	

Enter ARIEL *like a water-nymph*

Fine apparition! My quaint Ariel,
Hark in thine ear.

[*Whispers to Ariel*]

ARIEL	My lord, it shall be done.	*Exit*
PROSPERO	Thou poisonous slave, got by the devil himself	320
	Upon thy wicked dam, come forth.	

Enter CALIBAN

CALIBAN   As wicked dew as e'er my mother brushed
With raven's feather from unwholesome fen
Drop on you both! A south-west blow on ye,
And blister you all o'er!   325

PROSPERO   For this, be sure, tonight thou shalt have cramps,
Side-stitches that shall pen thy breath up; urchins
Shall, for that vast of night that they may work,
All exercise on thee; thou shalt be pinched
As thick as honeycomb, each pinch more stinging   330
Than bees that made 'em.

CALIBAN   I must eat my dinner.
This island's mine by Sycorax my mother,
Which thou tak'st from me. When thou cam'st first
Thou strok'st me and made much of me; wouldst give me
Water with berries in't, and teach me how   335
To name the bigger light, and how the less,
That burn by day and night. And then I loved thee
And showed thee all the qualities o'th'isle,
The fresh springs, brine-pits, barren place and fertile –
Cursèd be I that did so! All the charms   340
Of Sycorax – toads, beetles, bats – light on you!
For I am all the subjects that you have,
Which first was mine own king; and here you sty me
In this hard rock, whiles you do keep from me
The rest o'th'island.

Prospero accuses Caliban of attempting to rape Miranda. Miranda tells Caliban that he deserves to be imprisoned because he is evil. Caliban curses her but, fearful of Prospero's threats, obeys the order to leave.

1 Who speaks the lines? (in small groups)

Some people think that lines 351–62 are too harsh to be spoken by Miranda. In some productions, therefore, the lines are given to Prospero instead.

- If you were directing a stage production, who would you want to speak the lines – Miranda or Prospero? Write notes to prepare for a director's meeting in which you will advise the actors playing these characters. Remember to refer to the script in detail as you explain your decision about who speaks the lines.

Write about it

The official story? (by yourself)

What really happened when Prospero arrived on the island? Was Caliban an innocent, naturally good person whose genuine friendship towards Miranda was misinterpreted? Or was he a savage brute, tamed by Prospero, whose true nature came out when he tried to rape Miranda? Was Prospero a kind man who had no intention of seizing the island until Caliban's evil nature was revealed? Or was he deceitful and greedy, determined from the outset to exploit the island's natural resources and make Caliban his slave?

- Write an account of what you think happened, based on your knowledge of the characters in the play so far.

Characters

'You taught me language' (in pairs)

Line 363 raises very important questions about language and race. Throughout history, conquerors and governments have tried to suppress the language of certain groups that they believed to be inferior. Caliban expresses the resentment of the enslaved:

You taught me language, and my profit on't
Is, I know how to curse. The red plague rid you
For learning me your language.

- Search the script opposite (and elsewhere in this act) to find some of the curses Caliban uses. For each curse you find, write out what it means and try to find a modern equivalent.

---

stripes lashes

peopled … Calibans filled the island with my children

Abhorrèd hateful, frightful

print imprint, impression

capable of all ill naturally evil

purposes intentions, ideas

abide bear, endure

more than a prison (Miranda presumably means the death penalty, which was the punishment for rape)

curse (in the strong sense of a witch's curse)

red plague bubonic plague

rid destroy

learning teaching

Hag-seed son of a witch

answer other business respond to other tasks

rack torture

old cramps the pains of the aged

Setebos South American god

vassal slave

PROSPERO	Thou most lying slave,	345

Whom stripes may move, not kindness! I have used thee,
Filth as thou art, with humane care, and lodged thee
In mine own cell, till thou didst seek to violate
The honour of my child.

CALIBAN   O ho, O ho! Would't had been done.
Thou didst prevent me – I had peopled else   350
This isle with Calibans.

MIRANDA   Abhorrèd slave,
Which any print of goodness wilt not take,
Being capable of all ill! I pitied thee,
Took pains to make thee speak, taught thee each hour
One thing or other. When thou didst not, savage,   355
Know thine own meaning, but wouldst gabble like
A thing most brutish, I endowed thy purposes
With words that made them known. But thy vile race –
Though thou didst learn – had that in't which good natures
Could not abide to be with; therefore wast thou   360
Deservedly confined into this rock,
Who hadst deserved more than a prison.

CALIBAN   You taught me language, and my profit on't
Is, I know how to curse. The red plague rid you
For learning me your language!

PROSPERO   Hag-seed, hence!   365
Fetch us in fuel; and be quick, thou'rt best,
To answer other business. Shrug'st thou, malice?
If thou neglect'st, or dost unwillingly
What I command, I'll rack thee with old cramps,
Fill all thy bones with aches, make thee roar,   370
That beasts shall tremble at thy din.

CALIBAN   No, pray thee.
[*Aside*] I must obey; his art is of such power,
It would control my dam's god Setebos,
And make a vassal of him.

PROSPERO   So, slave, hence.

Exit Caliban

Ariel's first song is an invitation to dance upon the sands. Ferdinand is amazed by the music that has calmed both the storm and his grief. Ariel's second song describes a wonderful transformation after death.

1 Ariel's songs (in small groups)

Ariel's first song is about the calming of the tempest. It is an invitation to dance by the seashore where the waves kiss, becoming silent and calm. Ariel's second song tells how Alonso, the king, is magically transformed, having undergone 'a sea-change / Into something rich and strange'.

- Write a paragraph describing the kind of music you would choose to evoke the mood of these songs. Would it be harmonious and reassuring or eerie and slightly frightening?

Language in the play

The power of music (by yourself)

The language in the script opposite has several musical qualities: rhyme, rhythm and sound echoes all contribute to the musicality of this scene.

a Find examples of the following language features in the xcript opposite: **alliteration**; **rhyming couplets**; **onomatopoeia**; **personification** (see pp. 166–7 for more information on these).

b Choose one of Ariel's songs or Ferdinand's speech, and read it aloud two or three times. Then write a paragraph describing the effect of this language on an audience.

2 First sight of Ferdinand

Ferdinand says that the music has calmed his feeling of grief for his father, whom he believes drowned during the storm.

- Read Ariel's description of Ferdinand earlier in this scene (lines 221–4). Write down a few words to describe his appearance. Is he bedraggled or neatly dressed? Amazed or terrified? Then write a paragraph predicting what might happen to Ferdinand on the island.

Themes

Transformation (in pairs)

a Memorise the first six lines of Ariel's second song (lines 396–401) and identify all the transformations Alonso has undergone.

b What do you think Ariel means by a 'sea-change', and what emotions are evoked as you read these lines?

playing (probably the lute, a courtly instrument that allowed the player to accompany his own singing)

whist into silence

Foot it featly dance daintily, with graceful agility

the burden bear sing the chorus

dispersedly separately, not in unison

strain of strutting Chanticleer crowing of a proud cockerel (which recalls the boastful Chanticleer of Aesop's *Fables*)

waits upon attends

wrack shipwreck

Allaying calming
passion suffering, intense grief

Full fathom five at least 9 metres

fade decay

knell funeral bell

Enter FERDINAND, *and* ARIEL *invisible, playing and singing*

SONG

ARIEL   Come unto these yellow sands,   375
                  And then take hands.
                  Curtsied when you have, and kissed,
                  The wild waves whist.
                  Foot it featly here and there,
                  And sweet sprites the burden bear.   380
                        Hark, hark
                        The watch-dogs bark
                        Bow wow, bow wow.
                  [*Spirits dispersedly echo the burden 'Bow wow'*]
                        Hark, hark! I hear
                        The strain of strutting Chanticleer,   385
                        Cry cock-a-diddle-dow.
                  [*Spirits dispersedly echo the burden 'cock-a-diddle-dow'*]

FERDINAND   Where should this music be? I'th'air, or th'earth?
                  It sounds no more; and sure it waits upon
                  Some god o'th'island. Sitting on a bank,
                  Weeping again the king my father's wrack,   390
                  This music crept by me upon the waters,
                  Allaying both their fury and my passion
                  With its sweet air. Thence I have followed it –
                  Or it hath drawn me rather; but 'tis gone.
                  No, it begins again.   395

SONG

ARIEL   Full fathom five thy father lies,
                  Of his bones are coral made;
                  Those are pearls that were his eyes;
                  Nothing of him that doth fade,
                  But doth suffer a sea-change   400
                  Into something rich and strange.
                  Sea-nymphs hourly ring his knell.
                  Hark, now I hear them, ding dong bell.
                  [*Spirits dispersedly echo the burden 'ding dong bell'*]

Miranda wonders at Ferdinand, imagining him to be a spirit. Prospero assures her that Ferdinand is human. Ferdinand thinks that Miranda is a goddess, and is surprised to hear her speak his language.

Language in the play

A fairy-tale world? (in small groups)

Prospero's line 407 is a formal and elaborate way of saying 'open your eyes'. Prospero uses another elaborate image in lines 413–14.

- Take turns in role as Prospero, and describe why you are using such formal and solemn language. What effect are you hoping it will have on Miranda? How do you want her to respond to what she sees? Remember, Miranda is still in a dream-like state and is being invited to look at something new and strange.

1 'It goes on, I see'

Prospero's plan is working. Write an extended **aside** (see p. 168) for Prospero, to allow the audience to find out more about his desire to make Miranda and Ferdinand notice each other. Add at least four more lines to his aside in lines 418–19.

Stagecraft

How do you speak to a stranger? (in pairs)

With a partner, discuss how you think Ferdinand should speak and behave towards Miranda when he first sees her. Do you think the actor should be reminded that Ferdinand is a European prince who thinks that he is meeting a foreigner who doesn't speak his language? Or do you think this should be portrayed as a delicate moment, full of dream-like wonder?

◀ Write notes to the actors playing Ferdinand and Miranda, describing how you want them to behave during their first meeting.

---

ditty song
remember recall, commemorate
mortal human
owes owns
fringed … eye eyelids
advance raise, lift up

brave form handsome appearance

gallant young gentleman
but except that
canker corruption

these airs this music
Vouchsafe grant, graciously permit
remain live
bear me conduct myself
prime most important
maid human (not divine) or unmarried

best most noble (Ferdinand believes he is now king of Naples)

FERDINAND	The ditty does remember my drowned father.
	This is no mortal business, nor no sound 405
	That the earth owes. I hear it now above me.
PROSPERO	[*To Miranda*] The fringèd curtains of thine eye advance,
	And say what thou seest yond.
MIRANDA	What is't? A spirit?
	Lord, how it looks about! Believe me, sir,
	It carries a brave form. But 'tis a spirit. 410
PROSPERO	No, wench, it eats, and sleeps, and hath such senses
	As we have, such. This gallant which thou seest
	Was in the wrack; and but he's something stained
	With grief – that's beauty's canker – thou might'st call him
	A goodly person. He hath lost his fellows, 415
	And strays about to find 'em.
MIRANDA	I might call him
	A thing divine, for nothing natural
	I ever saw so noble.
PROSPERO	[*Aside*] It goes on, I see,
	As my soul prompts it. [*To Ariel*] Spirit, fine spirit, I'll free thee
	Within two days for this.
FERDINAND	[*Seeing Miranda*] Most sure the goddess 420
	On whom these airs attend. Vouchsafe my prayer
	May know if you remain upon this island,
	And that you will some good instruction give
	How I may bear me here. My prime request,
	Which I do last pronounce, is – O you wonder – 425
	If you be maid, or no?
MIRANDA	No wonder, sir,
	But certainly a maid.
FERDINAND	My language? Heavens!
	I am the best of them that speak this speech,
	Were I but where 'tis spoken.

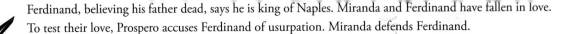

Ferdinand, believing his father dead, says he is king of Naples. Miranda and Ferdinand have fallen in love. To test their love, Prospero accuses Ferdinand of usurpation. Miranda defends Ferdinand.

1 Getting a word in – and not listening (in threes)

Ferdinand has fallen head over heels in love with Miranda, and he has eyes and ears for her alone. He is so entranced that Prospero finds it difficult to gain his attention.

a Read the script opposite and identify all the times Prospero asks Ferdinand for a 'word'. Notice how by line 451 Prospero seems to be getting exasperated: 'I charge thee / That thou attend me!'

b Create a tableau of these three characters as represented in the script opposite. Then create a second tableau that shows how Prospero is really feeling about the developing relationship between the young lovers.

Stagecraft

Staging the asides

There are three asides in the script opposite: two are spoken by Prospero and one by Miranda. Remember that an aside allows the character speaking to take the audience into his or her confidence, and gives the audience a greater understanding of what is happening than the other characters on stage.

- How would you ensure that the audience hears these asides, without the other characters on stage knowing what is going on? Sketch a diagram to show how you would position the actors. Use arrows and annotations to indicate their movement at this point in the play.

Themes

Does beauty equal goodness? (in pairs)

Is someone morally good because they are good-looking? Miranda thinks so. In lines 456–8, she says that Ferdinand's handsome face reflects his good character and that good drives out evil from beautiful people ('Good things will strive to dwell with't').

a Talk together about whether you believe a person's character shows in their face and general appearance.

b In role as Miranda, explain more fully what you mean in lines 456–8. Then script a response to her from Prospero, who probably has a different opinion and possesses a greater understanding of human nature than Miranda does.

How the best? in what way can you be the best?

single thing solitary, without family

Myself am Naples I am king
ne'er since at ebb always weeping

his brave son (this suggests that Antonio, 'the Duke of Milan', has a son, but no such person appears in the play)
twain two
braver excellent and worthy
control contradict
changed eyes fallen in love

I sighed for I loved

your affection … forth not in love with someone else

uneasy difficult
light (line 450) easy
light (line 451) cheap
usurp illegally seize
ow'st not do not own

PROSPERO	How the best?	
	What wert thou if the King of Naples heard thee?	430
FERDINAND	A single thing, as I am now, that wonders	
	To hear thee speak of Naples. He does hear me,	
	And that he does, I weep. Myself am Naples,	
	Who, with mine eyes, ne'er since at ebb, beheld	
	The king my father wracked.	
MIRANDA	Alack, for mercy!	435
FERDINAND	Yes, faith, and all his lords, the Duke of Milan	
	And his brave son being twain.	
PROSPERO	[*Aside*] The Duke of Milan	
	And his more braver daughter could control thee	
	If now 'twere fit to do't. At the first sight	
	They have changed eyes. [*To Ariel*] Delicate Ariel,	440
	I'll set thee free for this! [*To Ferdinand*] A word, good sir;	
	I fear you have done yourself some wrong; a word.	
MIRANDA	[*Aside*] Why speaks my father so ungently? This	
	Is the third man that e'er I saw; the first	
	That e'er I sighed for. Pity move my father	445
	To be inclined my way.	
FERDINAND	O, if a virgin,	
	And your affection not gone forth, I'll make you	
	The Queen of Naples.	
PROSPERO	Soft, sir, one word more.	
	[*Aside*] They are both in either's powers; but this swift business	
	I must uneasy make, lest too light winning	450
	Make the prize light. [*To Ferdinand*] One word more. I	
	charge thee	
	That thou attend me! Thou dost here usurp	
	The name thou ow'st not, and hast put thyself	
	Upon this island as a spy, to win it	
	From me, the lord on't.	
FERDINAND	No, as I am a man.	455
MIRANDA	There's nothing ill can dwell in such a temple.	
	If the ill spirit have so fair a house,	
	Good things will strive to dwell with't.	

Prospero threatens harsh punishment on Ferdinand, who draws his sword. Prospero freezes Ferdinand with a spell, and forces him to drop the sword. Prospero scolds Miranda for supporting Ferdinand.

1 'My foot my tutor?' – is Prospero angry? (in pairs)

Prospero's rebuke to Miranda is a vivid way of saying 'Shall something inferior presume to teach me?' Does Prospero speak impatiently and angrily, or with amused irony, or in some other tone? Is Miranda emotional and hysterical, or calming and appeasing?

- Read through lines 465–82 and experiment with different tones and emphases for this exchange between father and daughter.

Write about it

What is Ferdinand thinking?

We have seen Ferdinand shipwrecked, washed up on the island, weeping for his father (whom he believes to be dead), and overwhelmed by the beauty of Ariel's music. He then meets Miranda and falls in love with her, after which Prospero calls Ferdinand a spy and, at line 464, charms him from moving before imprisoning him.

- Write a diary entry for Ferdinand, in which he records these extraordinary events, how he feels about them, and his hopes and fears for the future.

▼ Find a line or stage direction from the script opposite that serves as a suitable caption for this picture (Ferdinand is on the right).

manacle chain

fresh-brook mussels inedible shellfish

entertainment treatment

too rash a trial too strong a test
gentle of high social status

mak'st a show pretends to be brave
Come from thy ward stop this sword-play
stick staff

surety guarantee

chide scold
advocate for supporter of

impostor liar, fraud
to compared to

goodlier handsomer

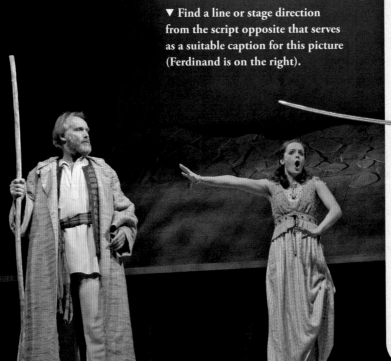

PROSPERO　　　[*To Ferdinand*]　　　　　　　　　　Follow me.
　　　　　　　[*To Miranda*] Speak not you for him: he's a traitor.
　　　　　　　　　[*To Ferdinand*] Come!
　　　　　　　I'll manacle thy neck and feet together;　　　　　　　460
　　　　　　　Sea water shalt thou drink; thy food shall be
　　　　　　　The fresh-brook mussels, withered roots, and husks
　　　　　　　Wherein the acorn cradled. Follow.

FERDINAND　　　　　　　　　　　　　　　No!
　　　　　　　I will resist such entertainment, till
　　　　　　　Mine enemy has more power.

He draws, and is charmed from moving

MIRANDA　　　　　　　　　　　　　O dear father,　　　　　　465
　　　　　　　Make not too rash a trial of him, for
　　　　　　　He's gentle, and not fearful.

PROSPERO　　　[*To Miranda*]　　　　　　What, I say,
　　　　　　　My foot my tutor? [*To Ferdinand*] Put thy sword up, traitor,
　　　　　　　Who mak'st a show, but dar'st not strike, thy conscience
　　　　　　　Is so possessed with guilt. Come from thy ward,　　　　470
　　　　　　　For I can here disarm thee with this stick,
　　　　　　　And make thy weapon drop.

MIRANDA　　　[*Kneeling*]　　　　　　Beseech you, father!
PROSPERO　　　Hence! Hang not on my garments.
MIRANDA　　　　　　　　　　　　　　Sir, have pity;
　　　　　　　I'll be his surety.

PROSPERO　　　　　　　　　Silence! One word more
　　　　　　　Shall make me chide thee, if not hate thee. What,　　　475
　　　　　　　An advocate for an impostor? Hush!
　　　　　　　Thou think'st there is no more such shapes as he,
　　　　　　　Having seen but him and Caliban. Foolish wench,
　　　　　　　To th'most of men this is a Caliban,
　　　　　　　And they to him are angels.

MIRANDA　　　　　　　　　　　　My affections　　　　　　480
　　　　　　　Are then most humble. I have no ambition
　　　　　　　To see a goodlier man.

Ferdinand says that, in spite of all his troubles, he will be content if he is allowed to see Miranda once a day from his prison. Prospero promises Ariel freedom in return for his services.

1 The romance tradition (in pairs)

The episode in this scene involving Ferdinand echoes two major elements of the romance and fairy-tale traditions that probably influenced Shakespeare as he wrote *The Tempest* (see p. 148).

* the harsh father who submits the young lover to trials and ordeals in order to test his love
* the power of love to overcome all suffering.

Find examples or quotations from the end of Act 1 Scene 2 that show both the trials of love and the power of love to overcome difficulties.

Stagecraft

Setting the scene

a Step into role as director and write notes for yourself, describing how you will present Act 1 Scene 2 from Ferdinand's entrance at line 375 to the end of the scene. Include reasons for your decisions about the style of this scene, the atmosphere you intend to create, and how you will stage particular dramatic moments. Pay special attention to the number of secret conversations that take place – between Prospero and Ariel and between Miranda and Ferdinand – as well as the asides that let the audience know more about what is happening on stage.

b Draw a rough sketch of a stage or use a plain piece of paper to mark out the characters' positions. Annotate your sketch and draw arrows to show how you want the characters to move and speak at every stage direction in the script opposite. For example, in line 492 for Prospero's aside 'It works', you might like to note that the actor should stay at the front of the stage and turn to the audience to allow only them to hear what he says.

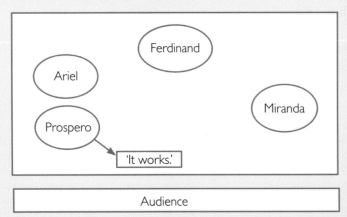

nerves muscles
in their infancy as weak as a baby

but light of little importance

All corners ... use of let other people have the rest of the world

unwonted unusual

PROSPERO [*To Ferdinand*] Come on, obey.
Thy nerves are in their infancy again
And have no vigour in them.

FERDINAND   So they are.
My spirits, as in a dream, are all bound up.   485
My father's loss, the weakness which I feel,
The wrack of all my friends, nor this man's threats,
To whom I am subdued, are but light to me,
Might I but through my prison once a day
Behold this maid. All corners else o'th'earth   490
Let liberty make use of; space enough
Have I in such a prison.

PROSPERO [*Aside*]   It works. [*To Ferdinand*] Come on!
[*To Ariel*] Thou hast done well, fine Ariel. [*To Ferdinand*]
     Follow me.
[*To Ariel*] Hark what thou else shalt do me.

MIRANDA [*To Ferdinand*]   Be of comfort;
My father's of a better nature, sir,   495
Than he appears by speech. This is unwonted
Which now came from him.

PROSPERO [*To Ariel*]   Thou shalt be as free
As mountain winds; but then exactly do
All points of my command.

ARIEL   To th'syllable.

PROSPERO [*To Ferdinand*] Come follow. [*To Miranda*] Speak not for him.   500

                                             Exeunt

Looking back at Act 1
Activities for groups or individuals

1 Challenging authority

Act 1 is full of challenges to authority. The Boatswain orders the king and courtiers to leave the deck. Prospero recounts how he was overthrown by his brother Antonio. Ariel and Caliban question Prospero's right to keep them as servants. Prospero accuses Ferdinand of wanting to take the island from him.

- In small groups, discuss each of these examples and decide whether or not the questioning of authority is justified. Then rank each example in order of most unlawful to least unlawful. Find quotations in the script to illustrate each of these challenges, and describe briefly why you have chosen your particular order.

2 Imprisonment

The relationship between imprisonment and powerlessness is a theme that runs through Act 1.

- Write two or three sentences about each of the characters listed below, explaining how they suffer imprisonment or confinement. Then develop your ideas into a paragraph, using embedded quotations. Explore who we feel the most sympathy for, and why.
  - Ariel
  - Caliban
  - Ferdinand
  - the crew of the shipwrecked vessel
  - Prospero and Miranda.

3 Prospero's overthrow

Neither television nor newspapers existed in Shakespeare's time. Imagine that they did. Show how *The Milan Times* or *Televisione Milano* reported the news of Prospero's overthrow and banishment by his brother Antonio. Remember that Antonio may have seized control of the media to ensure that his story is the only one that is heard. Choose whether you want to write for a broadsheet or tabloid paper, and give both the official and unofficial version in two reports.

4 Four stories – tell them, show them

In Scene 2, Prospero tells the story of how Antonio stole his dukedom (lines 66–168), and of Ariel's imprisonment by Sycorax (lines 25–93). Ariel describes how he brought about the shipwreck (lines 195–215). Caliban's story explains how he welcomed Prospero, but was condemned to slavery (lines 332–45).

- Prepare a series of three tableaux to depict one of these stories. Present your tableaux to the class and ask others to guess which story you are representing.

5 Caliban on stage

Look at the way in which Caliban has been presented in the photographs opposite. Is he a stereotype of a savage and deformed slave? Is he even human? How would you choose to portray Caliban on stage?

a Write a description of how you think he should look, move, sound and behave. Draw a sketch if you like, then collect pictures from magazines or draw pictures that represent ideas that you would like associated with him on stage. These could relate to his costume, the props he uses and his appearance.

b Refer back to descriptions of Caliban in the script at Act 1 Scene 2 lines 281–4 and lines 368–71. Note that in the first extract, it is not clear whether 'not honoured with / A human shape' refers to the island or to Caliban; Prospero may mean that except for Caliban, the island had no other human population. However, many directors have portrayed Caliban with some sort of deformity. How else might he be deformed and dehumanised on stage?

43

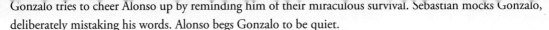

Stagecraft

'Beseech you, sir, be merry' (in pairs)

In the previous scene, Prospero praised Gonzalo for his kindness. Now the audience is reintroduced to this character through a carefully constructed opening speech. Gonzalo's lines here are written in **iambic pentameter** (see p. 165), with a deliberate and regular rhythm. Gonzalo is trying to lift the spirits of King Alonso, who is mourning the loss of his son, Ferdinand.

a Look closely at the arguments Gonzalo uses here. Talk together about how you think the actor should deliver lines 1–9.

b Read the rest of the script opposite. Discuss what you think each character wants here and how far they might go to get it.

1 A divided court?

Alonso's courtiers form two distinct groups. Gonzalo, Adrian and Francisco all attempt to comfort their king, trying to find good in what has happened to them. In contrast, Sebastian and Antonio comment cynically about what the others (and in particular Gonzalo) are saying.

a **Exploring character** In groups of six, take parts as Alonso and the five courtiers (remember that Francisco does not speak), and read lines 1–100. Sit or stand in two separate groups as you read, in order to emphasise the differences between the courtiers' characters (see also the photograph on p. 77).

b **Consumed by grief** In the first 100 lines of this scene, the character with the greatest authority – Alonso – speaks only five words. After you have read through this first section of the scene, discuss in groups where you would position this character. Should he overhear what is said by his courtiers, or should he stand apart from the rest of the group, unaware of what is taking place between them? How does he make his grief clear to the audience? In your Director's Journal, write down between five and ten notes for the actor. Then perform the first 100 lines of the scene, focusing on Alonso's role.

c **Mockery and sincerity** Divide into pairs and experiment with different ways of delivering the speeches in lines 1–100, ranging from mockery to despair. This will help bring out the sense and humour of the episode.

Beseech I beg

much beyond far greater than

hint cause, occasion

masters ... merchant owners of a merchant ship and the traders

weigh ... comfort balance our bad luck with the good luck of surviving

porridge stew of vegetables

visitor comforter of the sick

give him o'er so give up on him

One: tell it has struck one: keep count

When every ... offered if someone admits to every cause of grief

entertainer person who entertains grief

dollar a silver coin

Dolour sadness

spendthrift waster, chatterbox

I prithee, spare please be quiet

Act 2 Scene 1
A remote part of the island

Enter ALONSO, SEBASTIAN, ANTONIO, GONZALO, ADRIAN,
FRANCISCO *and others*

GONZALO	Beseech you, sir, be merry. You have cause –
	So have we all – of joy; for our escape
	Is much beyond our loss. Our hint of woe
	Is common; every day some sailor's wife,
	The masters of some merchant, and the merchant 5
	Have just our theme of woe. But for the miracle –
	I mean our preservation – few in millions
	Can speak like us. Then wisely, good sir, weigh
	Our sorrow with our comfort.
ALONSO	Prithee, peace.
SEBASTIAN	[*Apart to Antonio*] He receives comfort like cold 10 porridge.
ANTONIO	[*Apart to Sebastian*] The visitor will not give him o'er so.
SEBASTIAN	Look, he's winding up the watch of his wit,
	By and by it will strike.
GONZALO	[*To Alonso*] Sir, – 15
SEBASTIAN	One: tell.
GONZALO	When every grief is entertained
	That's offered, comes to the entertainer –
SEBASTIAN	A dollar.
GONZALO	Dolour comes to him indeed; you have spoken truer than you purposed. 20
SEBASTIAN	You have taken it wiselier than I meant you should.
GONZALO	Therefore, my lord –
ANTONIO	Fie, what a spendthrift is he of his tongue.
ALONSO	I prithee, spare.

Antonio and Sebastian mockingly bet on which courtier will speak first. They comment cynically on the optimistic remarks of the others. Gonzalo is amazed that everyone's clothes are clean and dry.

Themes

Utopia and dystopia (in threes)

After the shock of the shipwreck, Adrian and Gonzalo begin to notice how beautiful the island is. In contrast, Antonio and Sebastian only see the imperfections of the island on which they find themselves stranded.

- Is the island a utopia or a dystopia – a perfect society or a place where discontent and unhappiness reign? Discuss which view you agree with most.

1 Subjective and objective truth (in pairs)

Gonzalo continues to find the good points of the island, while Antonio and Sebastian see only the bad. Can they both be correct? Subjective truth is something that we believe to be true ('X is brilliant!'). Objective truth is what is clearly true ('The UK is in the Northern Hemisphere').

a Discuss the idea that subjective truth is the only truth that matters, and that objective truth is impossible to prove beyond doubt.

b Choose four objects in your classroom. One person in your pair points out only the positive features of the object, and the other only its negative features. Who is closer to the truth? Join with other pairs to debate the objective and subjective truths of these everyday objects. What conclusions do you reach?

c Now imagine that you have to explain the concept of objective and subjective truth to a class of younger children. Prepare a ten-minute lesson plan that uses lines from *The Tempest* to illustrate the differences between objective and subjective truth. You may want to consider episodes such as the storm, or characters such as Caliban. Use visual aids such as storyboarding to explain your ideas.

Stagecraft

One-word it! (in fours)

The dialogue in the script opposite moves very quickly. Try to make it even quicker, while retaining the sense of Shakespeare's script.

- First, cut back each line to a single word. Then act out the scene several times, choosing different ways of emphasising the words to create different effects.

wager bet

crow talk

A match! it's a bet!

desert uninhabited

you're paid by your laughter
you have won the prize

subtle gentle (Sebastian interprets it as 'crafty')

Temperance mild climate or a girl's name

save except

lush luxurious

lusty full of life

tawny brown, sunburnt

eye tinge

He misses not much he sees the smallest patch of green

he doth ... totally he gets everything completely wrong

rarity exceptional nature

credit belief

vouched rarities proclaimed wonders

garments clothes

notwithstanding in spite of that, nevertheless

glosses smart appearance

If but ... lies? if he checked inside his pockets, he would see he is wrong

GONZALO	Well, I have done. But yet –	25
SEBASTIAN	He will be talking.	
ANTONIO	Which, of he or Adrian, for a good wager, first begins to crow?	
SEBASTIAN	The old cock.	
ANTONIO	The cockerel.	30
SEBASTIAN	Done. The wager?	
ANTONIO	A laughter.	
SEBASTIAN	A match!	
ADRIAN	Though this island seem to be desert –	
ANTONIO	Ha, ha, ha!	35
SEBASTIAN	So: you're paid.	
ADRIAN	Uninhabitable, and almost inaccessible –	
SEBASTIAN	Yet –	
ADRIAN	Yet –	
ANTONIO	He could not miss't.	40
ADRIAN	It must needs be of subtle, tender and delicate temperance.	
ANTONIO	Temperance was a delicate wench.	
SEBASTIAN	Ay, and a subtle, as he most learnedly delivered.	
ADRIAN	The air breathes upon us here most sweetly.	45
SEBASTIAN	As if it had lungs, and rotten ones.	
ANTONIO	Or as 'twere perfumed by a fen.	
GONZALO	Here is everything advantageous to life.	
ANTONIO	True, save means to live.	
SEBASTIAN	Of that there's none, or little.	50
GONZALO	How lush and lusty the grass looks! How green!	
ANTONIO	The ground indeed is tawny.	
SEBASTIAN	With an eye of green in't.	
ANTONIO	He misses not much.	
SEBASTIAN	No, he doth but mistake the truth totally.	55
GONZALO	But the rarity of it is, which is indeed almost beyond credit –	
SEBASTIAN	As many vouched rarities are.	
GONZALO	That our garments being, as they were, drenched in the sea, hold notwithstanding their freshness and glosses, being rather new-dyed than stained with salt water.	60
ANTONIO	If but one of his pockets could speak, would it not say he lies?	
SEBASTIAN	Ay, or very falsely pocket up his report.	

Gonzalo continues to marvel at everyone's dry clothes. Antonio and Sebastian laugh sarcastically about Gonzalo's references to widow Dido and to the location of Carthage. Gonzalo again tries to cheer Alonso.

1 Exploring classical mythology

Gonzalo's lines 65–7 reveal that the court party was returning home from a wedding when the tempest struck. Alonso's daughter Claribel has married the king of Tunis.

Afric Africa

- **'widow Dido'** Dido, queen of Carthage, was a famous figure in Roman and Greek mythology. In one version of the myth, she was faithful to her dead husband. In another she had an affair with Aeneas, the Trojan prince who founded Rome, and she killed herself when he later abandoned her. Antonio and Sebastian's mockery may, therefore, lie in their amazement at hearing the tragic queen, who killed herself for love, described as 'widow Dido'.

paragon model of excellence

A pox o'that! nonsense!

- **'the miraculous harp'** Carthage was close to the city of Tunis (now in ruins). Antonio and Sebastian compare Gonzalo to the legendary Amphian, king of Thebes, who raised the city walls by playing his harp. Since Gonzalo mistakes Tunis for Carthage, Sebastian says Gonzalo has built the city out of words (line 83).

study of that think

To what extent do you think it is important for children to learn about ancient civilisations and their myths? Write a short article for your school magazine or website that argues either that such knowledge is important, or that it should make way for more 'relevant' subjects.

kernels seeds, pips

Characters

Who is telling the truth? (in pairs)

Knowledge is a key theme in *The Tempest*. Between lines 65 and 100, Gonzalo gives the impression of being very knowledgeable, but he is ridiculed by the other characters here for being misinformed.

rarest most beautiful
Bate except, leave out

- Discuss why you think Shakespeare chose to include these lines, and what they reveal about the characters who speak them. Can we still respect Gonzalo if he really is as misinformed as he appears? If Sebastian and Antonio are right, should we like and trust them more as characters?

doublet short jacket
in a sort in a way, relatively

GONZALO	Methinks our garments are now as fresh as when we put them on first in Afric, at the marriage of the king's fair daughter Claribel to the King of Tunis.
SEBASTIAN	'Twas a sweet marriage, and we prosper well in our return.
ADRIAN	Tunis was never graced before with such a paragon to their queen.
GONZALO	Not since widow Dido's time.
ANTONIO	Widow? A pox o'that! How came that 'widow' in? Widow Dido!
SEBASTIAN	What if he had said 'widower Aeneas' too?
ANTONIO	Good Lord, how you take it!
ADRIAN	[*To Gonzalo*] Widow Dido, said you? You make me study of that. She was of Carthage, not of Tunis.
GONZALO	This Tunis, sir, was Carthage.
ADRIAN	Carthage?
GONZALO	I assure you, Carthage.
ANTONIO	His word is more than the miraculous harp.
SEBASTIAN	He hath raised the wall, and houses too.
ANTONIO	What impossible matter will he make easy next?
SEBASTIAN	I think he will carry this island home in his pocket, and give it his son for an apple.
ANTONIO	And sowing the kernels of it in the sea, bring forth more islands.
GONZALO	Ay.
ANTONIO	Why, in good time.
GONZALO	[*To Alonso*] Sir, we were talking, that our garments seem now as fresh as when we were at Tunis at the marriage of your daughter, who is now queen.
ANTONIO	And the rarest that e'er came there.
SEBASTIAN	Bate, I beseech you, widow Dido.
ANTONIO	O widow Dido? Ay, widow Dido.
GONZALO	Is not, sir, my doublet as fresh as the first day I wore it – I mean, in a sort –
ANTONIO	That sort was well fished for.
GONZALO	– when I wore it at your daughter's marriage?

65

70

75

80

85

90

95

100

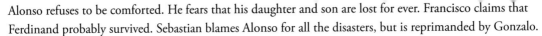

Alonso refuses to be comforted. He fears that his daughter and son are lost for ever. Francisco claims that Ferdinand probably survived. Sebastian blames Alonso for all the disasters, but is reprimanded by Gonzalo.

Stagecraft

Making the most of Francisco's speech

Lines 108–17 (and three words in Act 3 Scene 3, line 40) are Francisco's only words in the play. His description of Ferdinand swimming strongly is full of active verbs ('beat', 'ride', 'trod', 'flung', 'breasted', 'oared'). He paints an image of the cliff bending over, as if to help Ferdinand (lines 115–16).

- Imagine you are directing a production of *The Tempest*. In your Director's Journal, write a set of notes to the actor playing Francisco, offering advice on how to say these lines. Remember that this is his only chance in the play to make a memorable impression on the audience, so consider carefully how you want him to deliver his speech.

Themes

Sebastian challenges the king (by yourself)

In the script opposite, there is another example of a character challenging someone in a position of authority (see also p. 2). In lines 118–30, Sebastian strongly criticises Alonso, claiming that all the courtiers begged him not to permit the marriage of his daughter Claribel to the king of Tunis. Sebastian also asserts that Claribel did not want to marry the African king, but that – as a dutiful child – she obeyed her father's will. Alonso would not listen to either his courtiers or his daughter, with disastrous results.

a Read Sebastian's lines opposite carefully and identify the words or phrases that the actor could emphasise to hurt Alonso's feelings as much as possible.

b Write a paragraph explaining why you think Sebastian speaks harshly to his king here. What motivates him to be so cruel to a man who is obviously mourning the loss of both his son and his daughter?

in my rate in my opinion

mine heir (Ferdinand)

surges waves

surge most swol'n huge waves
contentious challenging
lusty powerful
his wave-worn basis the foot of the cliff

Who hath cause … on't who has cause to weep

kneeled to and impòrtuned begged

loathness unwillingness, hatred
beam scale, balance

time to speak it in occasion
plaster dressing for a wound

chirurgeonly like a surgeon

ALONSO You cram these words into mine ears, against
        The stomach of my sense: would I had never
        Married my daughter there. For coming thence
        My son is lost, and, in my rate, she too,
        Who is so far from Italy removed   105
        I ne'er again shall see her. O thou mine heir
        Of Naples and of Milan, what strange fish
        Hath made his meal on thee?

FRANCISCO   Sir, he may live.
        I saw him beat the surges under him,
        And ride upon their backs; he trod the water   110
        Whose enmity he flung aside, and breasted
        The surge most swol'n that met him. His bold head
        'Bove the contentious waves he kept, and oared
        Himself with his good arms in lusty stroke
        To th'shore, that o'er his wave-worn basis bowed,   115
        As stooping to relieve him. I not doubt
        He came alive to land.

ALONSO   No, no, he's gone.

SEBASTIAN Sir, you may thank yourself for this great loss,
        That would not bless our Europe with your daughter,
        But rather lose her to an African,   120
        Where she, at least, is banished from your eye,
        Who hath cause to wet the grief on't.

ALONSO   Prithee, peace.

SEBASTIAN You were kneeled to and impòrtuned otherwise
        By all of us; and the fair soul herself
        Weighed between loathness and obedience, at   125
        Which end o'th'beam should bow. We have lost your son,
        I fear for ever. Milan and Naples have
        More widows in them of this business' making
        Than we bring men to comfort them. The fault's
        Your own.

ALONSO   So is the dearest of the loss.   130

GONZALO My lord Sebastian,
        The truth you speak doth lack some gentleness,
        And time to speak it in; you rub the sore,
        When you should bring the plaster.

SEBASTIAN   Very well.

ANTONIO And most chirurgeonly.   135

1 'The noble savage' (whole class)

Here, Gonzalo further develops the theme of a utopia, or 'the golden age' (see p. 46). His picture of a society in which ownership of everything is shared ('commonwealth') is heavily influenced by an essay entitled 'On Cannibals', written by the French philosopher Michel de Montaigne (1533–92). Montaigne explored what it meant to be civilised, arguing that the 'savage' societies being

discovered in the New World (America) at the time were superior to the sophisticated civilisations of Europe. The essay (which Shakespeare read) gave rise to the belief in 'the noble savage', for whom harmonious, peaceful and equal relationships were completely natural.

- As a class, discuss what you think it means to be 'civilised' – as a human being, a community and a society. During this discussion, make notes in preparation for the activity below.

plantation colonisation
nettle-seed/docks/mallows weeds

contraries opposite to usual custom
Exècute organise
traffic trade, business
magistrate someone in charge of administration of the law
Letters literature, education
use of service slavery, servants
contract, succession inheritance
Bourn, bound of land, tilth boundaries, fences, agriculture
occupation employment
The latter … beginning the end of the speech seems to contradict its beginning
common for communal use

engine weapon

kind nature
foison plenty

minister occasion give opportunity
sensible and nimble sensitive and quick (mocking)

Write about it

Describing Utopia

Look at the things that Gonzalo would not permit in his utopian society, such as 'traffic' (trade and commerce) and 'letters' (education). What would be your utopia?

- Write an article for a magazine, outlining your own vision for a perfect society. Include a headline, then describe what would be included and forbidden in your utopia. Think carefully about the implications of each decision.
- Share your ideas with others in your class, then decide which society seems the most utopian. Are there any that you feel are the opposite of a perfect society (dystopian)?

GONZALO	[*To Alonso*] It is foul weather in us all, good sir,
	When you are cloudy.
SEBASTIAN	Foul weather?
ANTONIO	Very foul.
GONZALO	Had I plantation of this isle, my lord –
ANTONIO	He'd sow't with nettle-seed.
SEBASTIAN	Or docks, or mallows.
GONZALO	– And were the king on't, what would I do?
SEBASTIAN	'Scape being drunk, for want of wine.
GONZALO	I'th'commonwealth I would by contraries
	Exècute all things. For no kind of traffic
	Would I admit; no name of magistrate;
	Letters should not be known; riches, poverty,
	And use of service, none; contract, succession,
	Bourn, bound of land, tilth, vineyard, none;
	No use of metal, corn, or wine, or oil;
	No occupation, all men idle, all;
	And women too, but innocent and pure;
	No sovereignty –
SEBASTIAN	Yet he would be king on't.
ANTONIO	The latter end of his commonwealth forgets the beginning.
GONZALO	All things in common nature should produce
	Without sweat or endeavour. Treason, felony,
	Sword, pike, knife, gun, or need of any engine
	Would I not have; but nature should bring forth
	Of it own kind, all foison, all abundance
	To feed my innocent people.
SEBASTIAN	No marrying 'mong his subjects?
ANTONIO	None, man, all idle; whores and knaves.
GONZALO	I would with such perfection govern, sir,
	T'excel the Golden Age.
SEBASTIAN	'Save his majesty!
ANTONIO	Long live Gonzalo!
GONZALO	And – do you mark me, sir?
ALONSO	Prithee, no more; thou dost talk nothing to me.
GONZALO	I do well believe your highness, and did it to minister occasion to these gentlemen, who are of such sensible and nimble lungs, that they always use to laugh at nothing.
ANTONIO	'Twas you we laughed at.

Line numbers: 140, 145, 150, 155, 160, 165, 170

1 Gonzalo: sarcastic or annoyed? (in pairs)

It seems that the mild-mannered Gonzalo finally has enough of Antonio and Sebastian: he turns on them and attacks them for mocking him.

a Do you think Gonzalo shows genuine anger, or does he use a drier, more sarcastic tone? Given what you know of his character, which is the most likely? Discuss this with your partner.

b Experiment with ways of speaking everything Gonzalo says in lines 170–84, and decide on an appropriate style of delivery.

Characters

Antonio: opportunist or evil?

Up to this point, Antonio has come across as a rather mocking, cynical character in the play (remember Prospero's description of him in Act 1 Scene 2). However, at line 200 a more sinister side to him seems to emerge as he begins to tempt Sebastian into a murderous plot.

a Search the script opposite and the rest of Act 2 for evidence of Antonio's character. Do you think he is genuinely evil, or is he an opportunist who is doing what anyone else would do in his situation?

b Imagine that a director of the play wants to portray Antonio as an opportunist, but the actor playing him believes he should be depicted as a manipulative murderer. Write a record of their discussion in your Director's Journal, giving the arguments each one makes for their own interpretation of Antonio.

blow insult

And if

flat-long harmlessly (flat side of a sword)

brave mettle daring courage

sphere orbit

We would ... a-batfowling we would do that and then use the moon like a lantern to go catching birds by

warrant guarantee

adventure my discretion risk my reputation

heavy sleepy

I wish mine eyes ... thoughts I wish that closing my eyes would stop me thinking

omit ignore

heavy offer chance to sleep

nimble wide awake

consent agreement

Th'occasion speaks thee this is your opportunity

GONZALO   Who, in this kind of merry fooling, am nothing to you; so
      you may continue, and laugh at nothing still.   175

ANTONIO   What a blow was there given!

SEBASTIAN   And it had not fall'n flat-long.

GONZALO   You are gentlemen of brave mettle; you would lift the moon
      out of her sphere, if she would continue in it five weeks without
      changing.   180

Enter ARIEL [*invisible*] *playing solemn music*

SEBASTIAN   We would so, and then go a-batfowling.

ANTONIO   Nay, good my lord, be not angry.

GONZALO   No, I warrant you, I will not adventure my discretion so
      weakly. Will you laugh me asleep, for I am very heavy?

ANTONIO   Go sleep, and hear us.   185

[*All sleep except Alonso, Sebastian and Antonio*]

ALONSO   What, all so soon asleep? I wish mine eyes
      Would with themselves shut up my thoughts; I find
      They are inclined to do so.

SEBASTIAN   Please you, sir,
      Do not omit the heavy offer of it.
      It seldom visits sorrow; when it doth,   190
      It is a comforter.

ANTONIO   We two, my lord,
      Will guard your person while you take your rest,
      And watch your safety.

ALONSO   Thank you. Wondrous heavy.

[*Alonso sleeps.*]   [*Exit Ariel*]

SEBASTIAN   What a strange drowsiness possesses them?

ANTONIO   It is the quality o'th'climate.

SEBASTIAN   Why   195
      Doth it not then our eyelids sink? I find
      Not myself disposed to sleep.

ANTONIO   Nor I; my spirits are nimble.
      They fell together all, as by consent
      They dropped, as by a thunder-stroke. What might,   200
      Worthy Sebastian, O, what might? – No more.
      And yet, methinks I see it in thy face,
      What thou shouldst be. Th'occasion speaks thee, and
      My strong imagination sees a crown
      Dropping upon thy head.

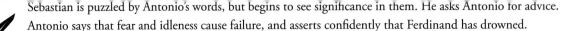

 Sebastian is puzzled by Antonio's words, but begins to see significance in them. He asks Antonio for advice. Antonio says that fear and idleness cause failure, and asserts confidently that Ferdinand has drowned.

Stagecraft

The plot thickens (in pairs)

Antonio has already seized his brother Prospero's throne. Now he begins to encourage Sebastian to do likewise – to usurp Alonso's throne.

a Take it in turns to read lines 194–293. Explore the different ways that these lines could be spoken by considering the following questions.

- Are there long pauses as Sebastian slowly realises that Antonio is prompting him to murder his own brother?
- Do they sit or stand face to face and make eye contact, or does Antonio deliberately avoid meeting Sebastian's gaze except at certain moments?
- How quickly does Sebastian realise what Antonio has in mind (be exact: find the line)?

b Act out the 'ebb and flow' of the conversation between Antonio and Sebastian. Consider the following:

- How might the actors physically show the shifting balance of power between the two characters?
- How does Sebastian's body language change when he realises what Antonio is proposing?

Language in the play

Exploring complex imagery (in pairs)

Lines 215–34 are rich in imagery. For example, Sebastian says he is like 'standing water' (line 217) – when the tide is about to turn and does not withdraw ('ebb') or go forward ('flow'). His own inclination is to ebb, and perhaps to even go backwards. Antonio replies that Sebastian's comparison is more powerful than he thinks, because unsuccessful men ('Ebbing men') are those who are fearful or idle.

a Pick out your favourite images in these lines and represent them visually, using pencil, pen, paint or a computer. You could try to storyboard the lines so that you create a coherent narrative with the words overlaying the images.

b Talk about your choices, considering the different ways that words and pictures convey the meaning of these lines.

waking awake

wink'st ... waking close your eyes (to this chance) while you are awake

if heed me if you take my advice
Trebles thee o'er makes you three times greater
standing water not ebbing or flowing

Hereditary sloth natural laziness

the purpose cherish hit the nail on the head

invest clothe
Ebbing unsuccessful

setting eager expression

throes thee hurts you

weak remembrance poor memory
as little memory as little remembered
earthed buried
spirit of persuasion chatterbox
only ... persuade his only job is to persuade

SEBASTIAN	What? Art thou waking?	205
ANTONIO	Do you not hear me speak?	

SEBASTIAN   I do, and surely
It is a sleepy language, and thou speak'st
Out of thy sleep. What is it thou didst say?
This is a strange repose, to be asleep
With eyes wide open; standing, speaking, moving,   210
And yet so fast asleep.

ANTONIO   Noble Sebastian,
Thou let'st thy fortune sleep – die rather; wink'st
Whiles thou art waking.

SEBASTIAN   Thou dost snore distinctly;
There's meaning in thy snores.

ANTONIO   I am more serious than my custom. You   215
Must be so too, if heed me; which to do,
Trebles thee o'er.

SEBASTIAN   Well: I am standing water.

ANTONIO   I'll teach you how to flow.

SEBASTIAN   Do so – to ebb
Hereditary sloth instructs me.

ANTONIO   O!
If you but knew how you the purpose cherish   220
Whiles thus you mock it; how in stripping it
You more invest it. Ebbing men, indeed,
Most often do so near the bottom run
By their own fear, or sloth.

SEBASTIAN   Prithee say on.
The setting of thine eye and cheek proclaim   225
A matter from thee; and a birth, indeed,
Which throes thee much to yield.

ANTONIO   Thus, sir:
Although this lord of weak remembrance, this,
Who shall be of as little memory
When he is earthed, hath here almost persuaded –   230
For he's a spirit of persuasion, only
Professes to persuade – the king his son's alive,
'Tis as impossible that he's undrowned
As he that sleeps here, swims.

SEBASTIAN   I have no hope
That he's undrowned.

Antonio predicts the fulfilment of Sebastian's greatest ambitions. Alonso's heir, Claribel, is so far distant that destiny itself invites Antonio and Sebastian to act. Sebastian recalls that Antonio overthrew Prospero.

Characters

Antonio – a sinister persuader (in pairs)

Antonio uses a number of different strategies to convice Sebastian to kill his brother:

- **Certainty** (lines 232–4) Despite Gonzalo's cheering words, Ferdinand is believed to be dead.
- **Ambition** (lines 235–9) Ferdinand's death opens up the opportunity for Sebastian's highest hopes to be fulfilled.
- **Hyperbole** (lines 242–6) Using extravagant exaggeration, Antonio claims that Claribel has no hope of succeeding to Alonso's throne. He claims she lives too far away ('beyond man's life'); only a messenger moving as fast as the sun could reach her ('unless the sun were post'); the journey would take as long as the time from a baby boy being born until he is ready to shave (notice that in lines 251–4, Sebastian summarises all Antonio has said, but stripped of the hyperbole). It is, he says, 'destiny' that this opportunity should arise.
- **Imagery** (lines 247–50) Antonio ends by using theatrical imagery – 'cast', 'perform', 'act', 'prologue', 'discharge'. Antonio declares the prologue is now history. It is up to them to decide how to perform the plot. As Sebastian begins to respond, Antonio makes his meaning plainer in lines 254–65.

a What does the script opposite tell us about Antonio's character? Discuss how his skilful use of language – especially rhetorical devices – manipulates Sebastian.

b Consider the motivation behind Antonio's speech, then add to the notes you began on page 56 advising the actor playing this character. How should he deliver these lines?

1 Good and bad angels (in threes)

If Antonio is behaving like Sebastian's bad angel, how could you balance this out by being his good angel?

- One of you plays Antonio, another Sebastian and the third takes on the role of an imaginary 'good angel'. Antonio and the good angel put forward their arguments for and against murdering Alonso.
  What does Sebastian stand to gain? And what does he stand to lose? Who does Sebastian find the most persuasive?
- Did other groups come up with different arguments from yours?

---

that way Ferdinand's way

pierce a wink … there imagine anything greater

Ten leagues thirty miles

note message

post messenger

too slow (the moon takes a month to complete a cycle)

cast thrown up

what's past the storm that made this possible

discharge performance

stuff matter

cubit arm's length

no worse … are in their sleep they resemble the dead

There … rule Naples you can be king

prate chatter

amply lengthily

chough jackdaw (talking bird)

content acquiescence

Tender like

supplant usurp, overthrow

ANTONIO   O, out of that 'no hope'   235
What great hope have you! No hope that way is
Another way so high a hope that even
Ambition cannot pierce a wink beyond,
But doubt discovery there. Will you grant with me
That Ferdinand is drowned?

SEBASTIAN   He's gone.

ANTONIO   Then tell me,   240
Who's the next heir of Naples?

SEBASTIAN   Claribel.

ANTONIO   She that is Queen of Tunis; she that dwells
Ten leagues beyond man's life; she that from Naples
Can have no note, unless the sun were post –
The man i'th'moon's too slow – till new-born chins   245
Be rough and razorable; she that from whom
We all were sea-swallowed, though some cast again –
And by that destiny, to perform an act
Whereof what's past is prologue; what to come
In yours and my discharge.   250

SEBASTIAN   What stuff is this? How say you?
'Tis true my brother's daughter's Queen of Tunis,
So is she heir of Naples, 'twixt which regions
There is some space.

ANTONIO   A space, whose ev'ry cubit
Seems to cry out, 'How shall that Claribel   255
Measure us back to Naples? Keep in Tunis,
And let Sebastian wake.' Say this were death
That now hath seized them, why, they were no worse
Than now they are. There be that can rule Naples
As well as he that sleeps; lords that can prate   260
As amply and unnecessarily
As this Gonzalo; I myself could make
A chough of as deep chat. O, that you bore
The mind that I do! What a sleep were this
For your advancement! Do you understand me?   265

SEBASTIAN   Methinks I do.

ANTONIO   And how does your content
Tender your own good fortune?

SEBASTIAN   I remember
You did supplant your brother Prospero.

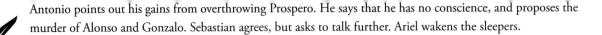

Antonio points out his gains from overthrowing Prospero. He says that he has no conscience, and proposes the murder of Alonso and Gonzalo. Sebastian agrees, but asks to talk further. Ariel wakens the sleepers.

Language in the play

Murderous words (by yourself)

Once again, authority is seen to be challenged on the island, but this time it takes on a much deadlier form. Antonio makes his plan clear: he will kill Alonso so that Sebastian can become king. Sebastian himself must kill Gonzalo to silence any criticism. Antonio implies that he has no conscience, and feels no sense of guilt for illegally seizing Prospero's crown.

a Identify the most striking images used by Antonio in this part of the scene. Write down why you think they are so effective.

b Identify the points in the script opposite where Antonio's mood and tone of voice become increasingly threatening.

c Bring together all the work you have done on Antonio and compose a letter to a well-known actor who you would like to play the part. Explain why you think he would be ideal as Antonio, and provide him with guidance about how to approach this character.

Stagecraft

Raising the tension

Ariel returns as the plotters are finalising their murderous plans. Explore ways of staging this part of the script so that the tension continues to rise. Take into account the points below, and try out some of the movements or gestures you would want the actors to use.

- Sound effects – what music or other sounds would you use here?
- Stage space – how would the actors use this?
- Lighting – would the lighting be changed in any way to reflect the growing seriousness of the situation?
- Pacing – does line 293 ('O, but one word') seem false? How can it be spoken convincingly?
- Movement, expressions and gestures – explore these to best represent Antonio, Sebastian and Ariel at this point.
- Costume and make-up – if you are able, dress up in costumes and make-up that identify the characters on stage. Try to reflect qualities such as each character's status and personality.

feater more elegantly

fellows equals

men servants

kibe sore, chilblain

deity … bosom God

candied coated with sugar

melt ere they molest unfreeze before they hurt

obedient steel dagger

lay … ever kill

doing thus doing the same

perpetual wink everlasting sleep, death

Should not upbraid if he is dead he will not be able to criticise

tell the clock … hour agree with our decision to act at an appropriate time

case example (usurping Prospero)

precedent example, model

got'st gained, seized

tribute protection money

art magic

project plan, purpose

ANTONIO	True;
	And look how well my garments sit upon me,
	Much feater than before. My brother's servants	270
	Were then my fellows, now they are my men.
SEBASTIAN	But for your conscience?
ANTONIO	Ay, sir: where lies that? If it were a kibe
	'Twould put me to my slipper; but I feel not
	This deity in my bosom. Twenty consciences	275
	That stand 'twixt me and Milan, candied be they,
	And melt ere they molest. Here lies your brother,
	No better than the earth he lies upon,
	If he were that which now he's like – that's dead;
	Whom I with this obedient steel, three inches of it,	280
	Can lay to bed for ever: whiles you doing thus,
	To the perpetual wink for aye might put
	This ancient morsel, this Sir Prudence, who
	Should not upbraid our course. For all the rest,
	They'll take suggestion as a cat laps milk;	285
	They'll tell the clock to any business that
	We say befits the hour.
SEBASTIAN	Thy case, dear friend,
	Shall be my precedent. As thou got'st Milan,
	I'll come by Naples. Draw thy sword; one stroke
	Shall free thee from the tribute which thou payest,	290
	And I the king shall love thee.
ANTONIO	Draw together:
	And when I rear my hand, do you the like
	To fall it on Gonzalo.
SEBASTIAN	O, but one word.

[They talk apart]

Enter ARIEL [*invisible*] *with music*

ARIEL	My master through his art foresees the danger
	That you, his friend, are in, and sends me forth –	295
	For else his project dies – to keep them living.

Sings in Gonzalo's ear

While you here do snoring lie,
Open-eyed conspiracy
　His time doth take.
If of life you keep a care, 300
Shake off slumber and beware.
　Awake, awake.

1 Unconvincing explanations? (in pairs)

Antonio and Sebastian are caught with swords in their hands. They have to provide a plausible explanation. Do they sound convincing?

a Explore ways of speaking lines 305–13 to show the two conspirators struggling to sound sincere. Try to bring out the element of humour as well as threat in these lines (for example, in some productions Sebastian makes the audience laugh at line 309 when he changes his story from 'bulls' to 'lions').

b Are there other moments in this scene in which Shakespeare uses humour to relieve the tension on stage?

▲ Sebastian (kneeling) and Antonio plot to kill the sleeping Alonso. Choose a quotation from the script opposite that would be a suitable caption for this picture.

sudden quick, violent

drawn with sword in hand
ghastly looking rightening appearance
securing your repose guarding you as you slept

humming music

cried shouted

verily true

Characters

'Heavens keep him from these beasts'

It is ironic that the dangerous 'beasts' that Gonzalo refers to are, in fact, the 'civilised' Antonio and Sebastian.

• In your opinion, who is the best advertisement for human nature on the island, and who is the least appealing? Choose your two characters and lists their strengths and weaknesses on a sheet of paper.

• Swap your list with a classmate and add to the points they have listed on their chosen characters. Explain your ideas with reference to the script. You will be able to use this work later, in your essay on this act (see p. 76).

ANTONIO	Then let us both be sudden.	
	[Antonio and Sebastian draw their swords]	
GONZALO	*[Waking]* Now, good angels preserve the king.	
	[He shakes Alonso]	
ALONSO	Why, how now? ho! Awake? Why are you drawn?	305
	Wherefore this ghastly looking?	
GONZALO	What's the matter?	
SEBASTIAN	Whiles we stood here securing your repose,	
	Even now, we heard a hollow burst of bellowing,	
	Like bulls, or rather lions; did't not wake you?	
	It struck mine ear most terribly.	
ALONSO	I heard nothing.	310
ANTONIO	O, 'twas a din to fright a monster's ear,	
	To make an earthquake. Sure it was the roar	
	Of a whole herd of lions.	
ALONSO	Heard you this, Gonzalo?	
GONZALO	Upon mine honour, sir, I heard a humming,	315
	And that a strange one too, which did awake me.	
	I shaked you, sir, and cried. As mine eyes opened,	
	I saw their weapons drawn. There was a noise,	
	That's verily. 'Tis best we stand upon our guard,	
	Or that we quit this place. Let's draw our weapons.	320
ALONSO	Lead off this ground, and let's make further search	
	For my poor son.	
GONZALO	Heavens keep him from these beasts:	
	For he is sure i'th'island.	
ALONSO	Lead away.	
ARIEL	Prospero my lord shall know what I have done.	
	So, king, go safely on to seek thy son.	325
	Exeunt	

Caliban curses Prospero, saying that Prospero's creatures control and torment him for the slightest offence. Fearing that Trinculo is one of Prospero's spirits, Caliban hides himself under his cloak.

Stagecraft

The first read-through (in threes)

Act 2 Scene 2 can be wonderfully funny both in the theatre and in a reading.

- To gain a first impression, take parts as Caliban, Trinculo and Stephano, and read straight through the whole scene. Don't pause to work out words you don't understand, but just enjoy the energy and humour of the scene. Take it in turns to read different parts if you like.

Themes

Justice and injustice (in threes)

Caliban first curses Prospero, then describes the ways in which Prospero torments him for every minor offence ('every trifle').

a One person takes the role of the narrator, and the two others play Caliban and Prospero. The narrator slowly reads lines 1–14, pausing after each torment (there are at least seven). In the pause, Caliban and Prospero argue about the 'crime' and the 'punishment'. To what extent do you think the crimes can be defended? And what do the actions of both characters tell us about them? Afterwards, talk together about whether Prospero or Caliban has the greatest cause for complaint.

b Improvise a trial between Prospero and Caliban, with a third person acting as the judge. Each character puts forward his 'case', defending his actions. At the end, the judge should reach a verdict of who is guilty of behaving badly.

1 'I needs must curse' (whole class)

Caliban's language is often powerful, and he uses provocative imagery despite knowing that Prospero's spirits (like secret police) are listening to his words. In fact, Caliban seems compelled to 'curse' his master. Why does he feel the need to do so when Prospero's punishments are so cruel?

- Discuss Caliban's determination to keep talking in defiance of Prospero. Why might his 'voice' and use of language be important in his struggle against his 'cruel' master? You could extend your discussion to include real-life examples of people who have spoken out against injustice despite attempts to silence them.

---

flats swamps
By inch-meal inch by inch

urchin-shows hedgehogs like demons or phantoms
firebrand ghostly light, will-o'-the-wisp
every trifle each small offence
mow make faces

wound entwined about

Perchance perhaps
mind notice

Act 2 Scene 2
Near Caliban's cave

Enter CALIBAN, *with a burden of wood. A noise of thunder heard*

CALIBAN   All the infections that the sun sucks up
From bogs, fens, flats, on Prosper fall, and make him
By inch-meal a disease. His spirits hear me,
And yet I needs must curse. But they'll nor pinch,
Fright me with urchin-shows, pitch me i'th'mire,   5
Nor lead me like a firebrand in the dark
Out of my way, unless he bid 'em; but
For every trifle are they set upon me,
Sometime like apes, that mow and chatter at me
And after bite me; then like hedgehogs, which   10
Lie tumbling in my barefoot way and mount
Their pricks at my footfall; sometime am I
All wound with adders, who with cloven tongues
Do hiss me into madness.

Enter TRINCULO

         Lo, now lo!
Here comes a spirit of his, and to torment me   15
For bringing wood in slowly. I'll fall flat,
Perchance he will not mind me.
     [*He lies down, and covers himself with a cloak*]

Trinculo is fearful of the weather. He discovers Caliban, and thinks of using him to make his fortune in England. Hearing thunder, Trinculo creeps under Caliban's cloak. Stephano enters, drunk and singing.

Characters

Trinculo and Stephano: a comedy double act (in pairs)

The introduction of two new characters who have escaped the shipwreck brings some much-needed comic relief. Trinculo is Alonso's court jester.

- Read Trinculo's lines and discuss how you would perform them. Is he rather stupid and scared of everything? Or is he in a state of post-traumatic shock, made worse by being in a strange new country? Would you play it purely for laughs (especially with lines such as 'What have we here …?' and 'Misery acquaints a man with strange bedfellows'). Or would you try to portray a darker, more complex character?

Write about it

Of monsters and men

The Elizabethan and Jacobean exploration of the Americas is strongly echoed in *The Tempest*. Explorers sometimes brought inhabitants of the newly discovered countries back to England. These 'Indians' were often cruelly displayed for profit in fairgrounds and other public places. The exhibitors made large profits from this inhuman practice ('There / would this monster make a man' means that Caliban would make him a large fortune).

- Imagine you are one of these captives in Shakespeare's England. Write a letter describing your experiences as a 'monster' on show. What stories can you tell?

1 Playing the drunk (in pairs)

Stephano is Alonso's butler or wine steward. He is very drunk, and he sings a rude song – one that contrasts greatly with Ariel's almost heavenly music.

- Even experienced actors find it difficult to play drunks convincingly. Before you attempt Stephano's song, discuss the challenges that such a part might involve. Remember that drunks are not necessarily loud and argumentative. Think about other convincing ways of interpreting this state.
- Consider not just the melody and tempo of the song, but also what it contributes to the scene overall.

bear off protect from

bombard large leather bottle

poor-John salted fish (hake)

painted advertised (painted on a board)

holiday-fool someone who attends holiday fairs

make a man … makes a man makes a man's fortune

doit small coin

Warm warm-blooded

o'my troth! by my faith!

suffered by been killed by

gaberdine cloak

bedfellows friends

shroud stay covered

dregs last drops

scurvy worthless

swabber deck-cleaner

tang sharp edge, serpent's tongue

Yet a tailor … itch a woman's tailor might have sexual relations with his clients

go hang! go to the devil!

TRINCULO   Here's neither bush nor shrub to bear off any weather at all, and another storm brewing – I hear it sing i'th'wind. Yond same black cloud, yond huge one, looks like a foul bombard that would shed his liquor. If it should thunder as it did before, I know not where to hide my head. Yond same cloud cannot choose but fall by pailfuls. [*Sees Caliban*] What have we here – a man, or a fish? Dead or alive? A fish, he smells like a fish; a very ancient and fishlike smell; a kind of, not-of-the-newest poor-John. A strange fish. Were I in England now – as once I was – and had but this fish painted, not a holiday-fool there but would give a piece of silver. There would this monster make a man; any strange beast there makes a man. When they will not give a doit to relieve a lame beggar, they will lay out ten to see a dead Indian. Legged like a man – and his fins like arms. Warm, o'my troth! I do now let loose my opinion, hold it no longer: this is no fish, but an islander, that hath lately suffered by a thunderbolt. [*Thunder*] Alas, the storm is come again. My best way is to creep under his gaberdine; there is no other shelter hereabout. Misery acquaints a man with strange bedfellows. I will here shroud till the dregs of the storm be past.

20

25

30

35

[*He hides under Caliban's cloak*]

Enter STEPHANO [*carrying a bottle and*] *singing*

STEPHANO   I shall no more to sea, to sea,
       Here shall I die ashore.
This is a very scurvy tune to sing at a man's funeral. Well, here's my comfort. (*Drinks*)

40

   (*Sings*) The master, the swabber, the boatswain and I,
      The gunner and his mate,
   Loved Mall, Meg and Marian, and Margery,
      But none of us cared for Kate.
      For she had a tongue with a tang,
      Would cry to a sailor, 'Go hang!'
   She loved not the savour of tar nor of pitch,
   Yet a tailor might scratch her where'er she did itch.
      Then to sea, boys, and let her go hang!
This is a scurvy tune too; but here's my comfort. (*Drinks*)

45

50

CALIBAN   Do not torment me! O!

Claiming to be brave, Stephano thinks of making a profit out of the four-legged 'monster'. Caliban cries out in fear. Stephano forces Caliban to drink, but is frightened by the sound of Trinculo's voice.

Stagecraft

Loud, grotesque – and funny (in fours)

Lines 59 to 85 are among the funniest in the play: they encourage the actors to emphasise the absurdity of the action, and to turn their characters into grotesques (exaggerated and unpleasant creatures).

- With one member of the group in role as director, experiment with this scene using an old coat or blanket to cover Trinculo and Caliban. Have a quick run-through, in which Stephano's words are slurred, and those of the other two characters – although inaudible and muffled – convey their mood. Don't forget that Caliban is getting drunk for the first time.
- After your practice session, perform your version of the scene to other groups.

Themes

Change and transformation

Caliban and Trinculo are transformed into something non-human here for comic effect. Transformation is one of the play's main themes, ranging from the sea becoming a destructive force, to sober men being transformed into drunks. What other signs of change and transformation can you identify in the play so far?

- On your own, write down as many examples of transformation as you can find.
- Discuss your ideas with a partner.
- Finally, share your jointly agreed points with the rest of the class.

68

STEPHANO   What's the matter? Have we devils here? Do you put tricks
upon's with savages and men of Ind? Ha? I have not 'scaped drowning to be afeared now of your four legs. For it hath been said, 'As
proper a man as ever went on four legs, cannot make him give   55
ground'; and it shall be said so again, while Stephano breathes at'
nostrils.

CALIBAN   The spirit torments me! O!

STEPHANO   This is some monster of the isle, with four legs, who hath
got, as I take it, an ague. Where the devil should he learn our lan-   60
guage? I will give him some relief if it be but for that. If I can
recover him, and keep him tame, and get to Naples with him, he's
a present for any emperor that ever trod on neat's leather.

CALIBAN   Do not torment me, prithee! I'll bring my wood home faster.

STEPHANO   He's in his fit now, and does not talk after the wisest. He   65
shall taste of my bottle. If he have never drunk wine afore, it will
go near to remove his fit. If I can recover him, and keep him tame,
I will not take too much for him; he shall pay for him that hath him,
and that soundly.

CALIBAN   Thou dost me yet but little hurt; thou wilt anon, I know it by   70
thy trembling. Now Prosper works upon thee.

STEPHANO   Come on your ways. Open your mouth; here is that which
will give language to you, cat. Open your mouth; this will shake
your shaking, I can tell you, and that soundly.

[Caliban drinks and spits it out]

You cannot tell who's your friend: open your chops again.   75

[Caliban drinks again]

TRINCULO   I should know that voice. It should be – but he is drowned,
and these are devils. O defend me!

STEPHANO   Four legs and two voices; a most delicate monster! His
forward voice now is to speak well of his friend; his backward voice
is to utter foul speeches, and to detract. If all the wine in my bottle   80
will recover him, I will help his ague. Come.

[Caliban drinks]

Amen. I will pour some in thy other mouth.

TRINCULO   Stephano.

STEPHANO   Doth thy other mouth call me? Mercy, mercy! This is a
devil, and no monster. I will leave him; I have no long spoon.   85

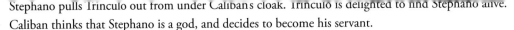

Stephano pulls Trinculo out from under Caliban's cloak. Trinculo is delighted to find Stephano alive. Caliban thinks that Stephano is a god, and decides to become his servant.

Themes

Appearance and reality (in pairs)

Shakespeare constantly explores the conflict between appearance and reality in *The Tempest* – perhaps no more so than here, where characters are 'transformed' from men into a strange creature (and back again). What appears to be the truth is often something quite different in this play.

* Identify parts of the script opposite where reality is not quite the same as the appearance. Think about the words, but also about how the characters might be dressed, and how they may behave. Are they completely open with each other?

siege excrement
moon-calf monster, idiot
vent excrete, throw out

constant settled
sprites Prospero's spirits
celestial heavenly
kneel to revere
butt of sack barrel of white wine

1 How important is context? (whole class)

As well as the theme of appearance and reality, this part of Act 2 Scene 2 brings together several other key ideas that recur throughout the play. The activity below will help you discover more about these themes.

a Divide the class into three large groups and allocate each group one of the topics below. In your groups, discuss the theme you have been allocated and answer the question in italics.

* **Imperialism and colonialism** (see pp. 154–5) Caliban's promise to serve Stephano loyally (lines 104–5) seems to echo what happened to Caliban when Prospero first came to the island.

  What is Shakespeare saying about the complex relationship between an indigenous population and an imperial force?

* **Historical sources** (see pp. 152–3) Stephano's story (lines 101–2) contains an echo of what happened during a real shipwreck that may have inspired Shakespeare to write *The Tempest*. In that shipwreck, too, the sailors heaved barrels overboard.

  How important is context to any interpretation of the play?

kiss the book swig from the bottle (a parody of swearing an oath on the Bible)
goose simpleton

* **Religion** Stephano's order to Trinculo and Caliban to 'kiss the book' (line 109) echoes the custom of kissing the Bible when promising to tell the truth, or vowing allegiance to a lord. This shows us how deeply embedded religion was in Shakespeare's England.

  How important are faith, spirituality and religion in this play?

b Each group should appoint a chairperson. After the initial group discussion, each chairperson should present the argument to the class that their group's theme is the most significant.

TRINCULO   Stephano! If thou beest Stephano, touch me, and speak to me; for I am Trinculo – be not afeared – thy good friend Trinculo.

STEPHANO   If thou beest Trinculo, come forth! I'll pull thee by the lesser legs. If any be Trinculo's legs, these are they.

[*Pulls him out*]

Thou art very Trinculo indeed! How cam'st thou to be the siege of   90
this moon-calf? Can he vent Trinculos?

TRINCULO   I took him to be killed with a thunder-stroke. But art thou not drowned, Stephano? I hope now thou art not drowned. Is the storm over-blown? I hid me under the dead moon-calf's gaberdine for fear of the storm. And art thou living, Stephano? O Stephano,   95
two Neapolitans 'scaped!

[*Embraces Stephano*]

STEPHANO   Prithee do not turn me about, my stomach is not constant.

CALIBAN   [*Aside*] These be fine things, and if they be not sprites. That's a brave god, and bears celestial liquor. I will kneel to him.

STEPHANO   How didst thou 'scape? How cam'st thou hither? Swear by   100
this bottle how thou cam'st hither. I escaped upon a butt of sack which the sailors heaved o'erboard, by this bottle – which I made of the bark of a tree, with mine own hands, since I was cast ashore.

CALIBAN   I'll swear upon that bottle to be thy true subject, for the liquor is not earthly.   105

STEPHANO   Here. Swear then how thou escap'dst.

TRINCULO   Swum ashore, man, like a duck. I can swim like a duck, I'll be sworn.

STEPHANO   [*Gives bottle to Trinculo*] Here, kiss the book. Though thou canst swim like a duck, thou art made like a goose.   110

TRINCULO   O Stephano, hast any more of this?

STEPHANO   The whole butt, man. My cellar is in a rock by the sea-side, where my wine is hid. [*To Caliban*] How now, moon-calf, how does thine ague?

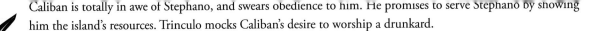

Caliban is totally in awe of Stephano, and swears obedience to him. He promises to serve Stephano by showing him the island's resources. Trinculo mocks Caliban's desire to worship a drunkard.

Characters

Caliban: the human and the inhuman

Stephano and Trinculo do not regard Caliban as a human being like themselves. In one production, Caliban appeared in later scenes with a placard around his neck that read 'Monster' (see the picture on p. 86).

a List all the names that Stephano and Trinculo call Caliban in Scene 2. As you read the rest of the play, add to this list and keep a tally of how many times they refer to him as 'monster'.

b What advice would you give the actor playing Caliban here? How should he both conform to the imagery used by Stephano and Trinculo and retain his humanity? What advice might you give the other actors in this scene – how should they interac with Caliban and with one another?

c Write a psychologist's report on each of the three characters in the script opposite, in which you describe and explain their behaviour. What should they work to change about themselves? Why do they need to change? What do you predict will happen if they don't?

1 A tour of the island (in fours)

- Create a presentation based on lines 137–49, in which you map out the island. In particular, think about where all the characters are situated at this point in the play, while Caliban is pledging his loyalty to Stephano, and note their positions. You can use anything from a computer program to pencils, pens and paint, but make sure it is 'an isle full of noises, sounds and sweet airs',
as well as a place of imprisonment and danger.

- Give the rest of the class a guided tour around your version of the island. As one person presents, the other three take parts as Caliban, Stephano and Trinculo. and act out lines 137–49.

Out o'th'moon from another world (some early settlers in the New World claimed to the native people that they were gods from the moon)

when time was once upon a time

My mistress (Miranda)

thy dog … bush your dog and the kindling (a proverb that says the man in the moon was banished there for collecting kindling on Sunday)

furnish it anon fill it soon

this good light the sun

shallow lacking depth of intelligence and character

credulous gullible, foolish

drawn swallowed

sooth faith

kiss thy foot obey you

puppy-headed dog-brained, stupid

in drink drunk

CALIBAN   Hast thou not dropped from heaven?   115

STEPHANO   Out o'th'moon I do assure thee. I was the man i'th'moon,
when time was.

CALIBAN   I have seen thee in her; and I do adore thee. My mistress
showed me thee, and thy dog, and thy bush.

STEPHANO   Come, swear to that! [*Giving him the bottle*] Kiss the book   120
– I will furnish it anon with new contents. Swear.

[*Caliban drinks*]

TRINCULO   [*Aside*] By this good light, this is a very shallow monster. I
afeared of him? A very weak monster. The man i'th'moon? A most
poor, credulous monster. Well drawn, monster, in good sooth.

CALIBAN   I'll show thee every fertile inch o'th'island. And I will kiss thy   125
foot – I prithee be my god.

TRINCULO   [*Aside*] By this light, a most perfidious and drunken monster
– when's god's asleep he'll rob his bottle.

CALIBAN   I'll kiss thy foot; I'll swear myself thy subject.

STEPHANO   Come on then: down and swear.   130

TRINCULO   [*Aside*] I shall laugh myself to death at this puppy-headed
monster. A most scurvy monster. I could find in my heart to beat
him –

STEPHANO   [*To Caliban*] Come, kiss.

TRINCULO   – but that the poor monster's in drink. An abominable   135
monster.

CALIBAN   I'll show thee the best springs; I'll pluck thee berries;
   I'll fish for thee, and get thee wood enough.
   A plague upon the tyrant that I serve!
   I'll bear him no more sticks, but follow thee,   140
   Thou wondrous man.

TRINCULO   [*Aside*] A most ridiculous monster, to make a wonder of a
poor drunkard.

1 Still a slave

Many productions use Caliban's song as an opportunity for a joyous exit from the stage. Very often, Stephano and Trinculo join in the singing. Caliban's shout of 'Freedom' is ironic, since he has simply exchanged one master for another.

- Consider whether you think the audience should laugh at Caliban, or feel sorry for him as he becomes drunk.

- Stage the final moments of the scene to show as clearly as possible that Caliban has not found freedom – he has simply become the slave of a different master.

crabs crab-apples

pig-nuts ground-nuts

marmoset small monkey

clust'ring filberts bunches of hazelnuts

scamels (possibly) seashells

all our company else our other companions

inherit here become rulers of the island

we'll fill him we'll fill the bottle

by and by immediately

firing firewood

At requiring as commanded

scrape trencher scrub wooden plates

get a new man Prospero can get a new servant

high-day liberty, holiday

CALIBAN   I prithee let me bring thee where crabs grow;
            And I with my long nails will dig thee pig-nuts,   145
            Show thee a jay's nest, and instruct thee how
            To snare the nimble marmoset. I'll bring thee
            To clust'ring filberts, and sometimes I'll get thee
            Young scamels from the rock. Wilt thou go with me?

STEPHANO   I prithee, now lead the way without any more talking. Trin-   150
           culo, the king and all our company else being drowned, we will
           inherit here. [*To Caliban*] Here; bear my bottle. Fellow Trinculo,
           we'll fill him by and by again.

CALIBAN   (*Sings drunkenly*) Farewell, master; farewell, farewell.

TRINCULO A howling monster; a drunken monster.   155

CALIBAN   [*Singing*] No more dams I'll make for fish,
                     Nor fetch in firing
                     At requiring,
                 Nor scrape trencher, nor wash dish,
                     Ban, ban, Ca-caliban   160
                 Has a new master – get a new man.
           Freedom, high-day, high-day freedom, freedom high-day, freedom.

STEPHANO   O brave monster, lead the way!

                                                               Exeunt

Looking back at Act 2
Activities for groups or individuals

1 A mini Act 2

A great deal happens in Act 2, but what are the most important moments? The following activity will help you decide.

- Write out (in continuous prose) the main action and ideas that take place in this act. You must do this in exactly 200 words.
- In pairs, compare your work and agree on which 100 words you would cut and which you would leave. Together, rewrite the remaining action in exactly 100 words.
- Next, cut down this draft to fifty words. Make sure your text remains clear and fluent.
- Cut down these fifty words into a twenty-five word mini summary of Act 2. Read this to the rest of the class.
- Finally, cut down these twenty-five words to a single word that best sums up Act 2. Take it turns to go to a board and write or pin up that word. Then explain your choice and make a note of the ideas behind the other word choices.
- You might try reversing this activity: begin with one word and build it up to 200 words.

2 What is Prospero thinking?

Prospero does not appear in Act 2. However, he uses Ariel to prevent murder in Scene 1, and Caliban's first song in Scene 2 refers to Prospero's 'spirits' following him.

- In groups, imagine that you are these sprites reporting back to Prospero after every scene. Would you portray them as fairies, secret police, children, resentful slaves, or something else? How would you describe what is happening? How do you think Prospero would respond? To what extent is he in charge of them?

3 What does it mean to be civilised?

Act 2 Scene 1 reveals the murderous intentions of the 'civilised' Antonio and Sebastian. Scene 2, which shows Caliban's encounter with Stephano and Trinculo, reflects what happened when Europeans colonised the Americas. The Europeans assumed that they were superior to the native people; they tried to make money out of them, drugged them with alcohol, and made them their servants.

- As a class, discuss whether or or not you think Shakespeare is using Act 2 to make ironic and critical comments on colonisation and 'civilisation' (see p. 154 for more information about this).
- Consider the qualities that you think make an individual – and a society – 'civilised'. Debate as a class and agree on a list of ten qualities.
- Afterwards, return to *The Tempest* – how many of these ten qualities can you find in the script, and who is most closely associated with them?

4 Imprisoned women

We have been 'introduced' to three female characters: Sycorax, Claribel and Miranda (though only the last is seen on stage). Although very different, they seem to share one similarity: they are all restricted or imprisoned, and their fates are decided by men.

- In pairs, discuss why you think Shakespeare has done this and whether it reveals more about the male characters or the female ones.

5 Who has rightful authority?

Act 2 continues to explore the theme of rightful authority.

- Using the notes you have compiled so far, write an essay – using embedded quotations – discussing this theme as it is presented in both Act 1 and Act 2. Remember to plan your essay before you write it.

The Tempest has been adapted for film many times in modern dress. In this 2010 production, we see Alonso, Sebastian, Gonzalo and Antonio exploring the island after surviving the storm.

Ferdinand reflects that his hard labour is pleasurable, because thoughts of Miranda make the work enjoyable. Miranda pleads with him to rest. She says that the logs will weep for Ferdinand as they burn.

1 A 'mean task' (by yourself)

Prospero forces Ferdinand to do exactly the same wood-carrying task as Caliban. Although he is forced to work as a slave, Ferdinand says that this social degradation is a noble task for the sake of Miranda. How is Ferdinand's response different to Caliban's?

- Imagine Caliban is secretly watching and listening to Ferdinand's speech here. Write out what is going through his head. Refer to specific parts of the script opposite as you try to capture Caliban's tone and perspective.

Language in the play

Weigh the contrasts (in pairs)

Conflict is central to all drama, and Shakespeare uses **antitheses** (see 'The language of *The Tempest*', p. 167) throughout this play as a way of expressing contrasts or conflicts. Lines 1–9 contain at least eight contrasts.

a Stand opposite each other and read the lines aloud. Every time Ferdinand makes a contrast, such as 'sports' versus 'painful' or 'labour' versus 'delight', swap places with your partner.

b Read through these lines again. This time, instead of swapping places, devise gestures or movements that embody this conflict. Pay attention to what your partner's body movement conveys about the conflict in each instance.

c Afterwards, talk together about why conflict is so important to drama in general.

---

sports recreational activities
painful difficult, laborious
sets off cancels, removes
baseness hard labour
heavy wearisome
odious hateful
but except that
quickens brings to life
crabbed harsh and irritable

sore injunction strict command
such baseness ... like executor such low-grade work never had so noble a workman
I forget (Ferdinand has stopped work, but resumes carrying the logs at this point)
Most busy ... do it Miranda fills my mind as I work

enjoined ordered, forced
burns ... weep (Miranda refers to the way that wood exudes drops of resin as it burns, and imagines it weeping)
safe not likely to come out or intervene

Act 3 Scene 1

Near Prospero's cave

Enter FERDINAND, *bearing a log*

FERDINAND   [*Sets down the log*] There be some sports are painful, and
       their labour
     Delight in them sets off. Some kinds of baseness
     Are nobly undergone; and most poor matters
     Point to rich ends. This my mean task would be
     As heavy to me as odious, but   5
     The mistress which I serve quickens what's dead,
     And makes my labours pleasures. O, she is
     Ten times more gentle than her father's crabbed –
     And he's composed of harshness. I must remove
     Some thousands of these logs, and pile them up,   10
     Upon a sore injunction. My sweet mistress
     Weeps when she sees me work, and says such baseness
     Had never like executor. I forget. [*Picks up the log*]
     But these sweet thoughts do even refresh my labours,
     Most busy, least when I do it.   15

Enter MIRANDA, *and* PROSPERO [*following at a distance*]

MIRANDA   Alas, now pray you
     Work not so hard. I would the lightning had
     Burnt up those logs that you are enjoined to pile.
     Pray set it down, and rest you. When this burns
     'Twill weep for having wearied you. My father   20
     Is hard at study; pray now, rest yourself –
     He's safe for these three hours.

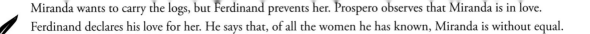

Miranda wants to carry the logs, but Ferdinand prevents her. Prospero observes that Miranda is in love. Ferdinand declares his love for her. He says that, of all the women he has known, Miranda is without equal.

1 Catching the plague of love (by yourself)

Prospero's lines 32–3 compare falling in love with catching a disease ('visitation' means a visit of the plague). A modern equivalent is the phrase 'You've got it bad'. Does Miranda share her father's view of love?

- Write out how you think Miranda would respond if she overheard her father say 'Poor worm, thou art infected'. Refer to the script and use your understanding of Miranda's character and experiences.

Characters

'Admired Miranda'

Miranda disobeys her father's order and tells Ferdinand her name. In Latin, 'Miranda' means 'to be wondered at'. If you turn back to the young lovers' first meeting, you will find that Ferdinand calls her 'O you wonder' (Act 1 Scene 2, line 425). Ferdinand plays with this meaning in 'Admired' and 'admiration' (lines 38–9). He is punning on the Latin meaning of her name and using **polyptoton** (the repetition of words from the same root but with different endings).

- Try using language in the same way with the names of other characters. Write a sentence each punning on 'Prospero', 'Caliban', 'Sycorax' and 'Ariel'. Refer to some aspect of their character or circumstances. You might like to imitate the way Ferdinand plays on the meaning of Miranda's name, or you could build your pun around a particular quality that a character demonstrates.

2 Playing with absolute sincerity (in pairs)

This is what one actor who played Ferdinand said about lines 38–49:

Ferdinand has been captivated by many women, but found some fault in every one. Only Miranda is perfect. You have to play these lines absolutely sincerely, full of wonder. Although it's not the kind of language you hear nowadays, you can make it ring true. Your job is to convince the audience you are really in love for the first time. You simply mustn't be embarrassed. The same applies to Miranda's lines too.

- Take the actor's advice as your cue to practise speaking as Ferdinand and Miranda. If you are embarrassed, talk about why this part of the script prompts such a response. Why might Shakespeare have given the characters such language at this point in the play?

---

discharge finish, complete

crack strain

become me suit me

good will … against I am well disposed to the task, whereas it offends you
Poor worm (Prospero uses an affectionate expression for Miranda)
infected in love ('you've caught it')
visitation visit (like a disease)

hest command

dearest most valuable

into bondage … ear captured (captivated) me
too diligent over-attentive

put it to the soil besmirched it
peerless without equal

FERDINAND   O most dear mistress,
The sun will set before I shall discharge
What I must strive to do.

MIRANDA   If you'll sit down
I'll bear your logs the while. Pray give me that;   25
I'll carry it to the pile.

FERDINAND   No, precious creature,
I'd rather crack my sinews, break my back,
Than you should such dishonour undergo,
While I sit lazy by.

MIRANDA   It would become me
As well as it does you; and I should do it   30
With much more ease, for my good will is to it,
And yours it is against.

PROSPERO   [*Aside*]   Poor worm, thou art infected;
This visitation shows it.

MIRANDA   You look wearily.

FERDINAND   No, noble mistress, 'tis fresh morning with me
When you are by at night. I do beseech you   35
Chiefly, that I might set it in my prayers,
What is your name?

MIRANDA   Miranda. – O my father,
I have broke your hest to say so.

FERDINAND   Admired Miranda,
Indeed the top of admiration, worth
What's dearest to the world. Full many a lady   40
I have eyed with best regard, and many a time
Th'harmony of their tongues hath into bondage
Brought my too diligent ear. For several virtues
Have I liked several women, never any
With so full soul but some defect in her   45
Did quarrel with the noblest grace she owed,
And put it to the soil. But you, O you,
So perfect and so peerless, are created
Of every creature's best.

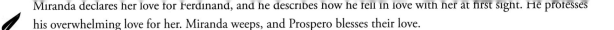

Miranda declares her love for Ferdinand, and he describes how he fell in love with her at first sight. He professes his overwhelming love for her. Miranda weeps, and Prospero blesses their love.

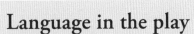

Language in the play
Verse and prose

Ferdinand and Miranda talk together in a way that no one uses in conversation today. Their elaborate verse seems to come from a fairy-tale world. Miranda's speech in lines 49–58 is particularly formal. Where Ferdinand bases his compliments on his experience of women, she praises him from her contrasting ignorance of men.

* Rewrite the verse opposite as prose (for either character) and try to capture the essence of what they say in modern English. As a class, listen to one another's examples and discuss the different effects of verse and prose.

1 Which images can you 'see'? (by yourself)

Which of the following images from the script opposite do you find easy to visualise? Write them in order, ranging from the easiest to the most difficult. Alongside each image, write about the picture it conjures up in your mind.

* 'The jewel in my dower' (line 55)
* 'This wooden slavery' (line 64)
* 'The flesh-fly blow my mouth' (line 65)
* 'My heart fly to your service' (line 67)
* 'patient log-man' (line 69)
* 'Heavens rain grace / On that which breeds between 'em' (lines 77–8).

Write about it
Casting for Miranda

* Look at the pictures of Miranda on pages viii, 18, 34, 38, 123, 134, 160 and 161. Which comes closest to your view of her? In role as director of a new performance, describe the kind of actress you would want to play Miranda. Think about her age, her appearance, her mannerisms and her previous roles. You may even want a specific actress whom you already admire or who has specific skills or talents.
* Write notes as a casting director, asking one of your assistants to search the agencies on the Internet, or drama schools' websites, to see if they can find someone suitable.

---

glass mirror

How features are abroad
what men look like elsewhere

skilless ignorant

modesty chastity

The jewel in my dower
my most precious possession

prattle / Something too wildly
speak too freely and
too much

precepts orders

condition rank, social status

wooden slavery log-carrying

suffer endure, permit

flesh-fly fly that lays its eggs in
dead flesh

blow my mouth deposit its eggs
in my mouth

patient long-suffering or diligent

kind event happy outcome

if hollowly … mischief
if I lie, change my good fortune
to bad

what whatever

MIRANDA   I do not know
             One of my sex; no woman's face remember,   50
             Save from my glass, mine own. Nor have I seen
             More that I may call men than you, good friend,
             And my dear father. How features are abroad
             I am skilless of; but by my modesty,
             The jewel in my dower, I would not wish   55
             Any companion in the world but you;
             Nor can imagination form a shape
             Besides yourself, to like of. But I prattle
             Something too wildly, and my father's precepts
             I therein do forget.   60

FERDINAND   I am in my condition
             A prince, Miranda; I do think a king –
             I would not so – and would no more endure
             This wooden slavery than to suffer
             The flesh-fly blow my mouth. Hear my soul speak.   65
             The very instant that I saw you, did
             My heart fly to your service, there resides
             To make me slave to it, and for your sake
             Am I this patient log-man.

MIRANDA   Do you love me?

FERDINAND   O heaven, O earth, bear witness to this sound,   70
             And crown what I profess with kind event
             If I speak true; if hollowly, invert
             What best is boded me to mischief. I,
             Beyond all limit of what else i'th'world,
             Do love, prize, honour you.

MIRANDA   I am a fool   75
             To weep at what I'm glad of.

PROSPERO   [*Aside*]   Fair encounter
             Of two most rare affections. Heavens rain grace
             On that which breeds between 'em.

FERDINAND   Wherefore weep you?

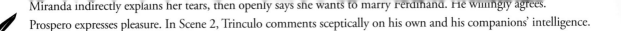
Language in the play

Riddles, plain speech and images of fertility

In lines 79–83, Miranda explains in an enigmatic way why she is weeping. She dare not offer what she wants to give (herself), but cannot live without what she lacks (Ferdinand). She decides to speak directly ('this is trifling', 'Hence, bashful cunning') and offers herself as wife to Ferdinand.

Some critics have noted that Miranda uses an image of pregnancy to describe how she speaks initially in riddles: 'the more it seeks to hide itself / The bigger bulk it shows.' Ferdinand also uses language that implies growth and abundance in line 93.

a Write a paragraph describing how the language used here reflects the growing love between Miranda and Ferdinand. Consider the formal verse used earlier and the fruitful language of growth and abundance in the script opposite.

b Use the Internet to help you compare the formal speeches given by Miranda and Ferdinand with other romantic love poetry written around the same time, such as that by Philip Sidney or John Donne. You could also compare it with less romantic poems, such as 'Come live with me and be my love' by Christopher Marlowe (look also for Sir Walter Raleigh's reply).

Stagecraft

Stage directions in the language (in pairs)

How many implied stage directions can you find in the lovers' pledge and farewell (lines 85–93)? At each of these points, write a detailed and explicit stage direction to advise the actors playing the parts of Miranda and Ferdinand.

1 A sneak preview of Scene 2 (in threes)

a Take parts and read through the whole of Scene 2. Remember – all three men have been drinking heavily, and can probably barely stand.

b Work out how you would stage the scene, identifying the lines where you would attempt to get the loudest laughs from the audience. For example, Trinculo's sceptical statement in lines 5–6 ('if th'other / two be brained like us, the state totters') usually evokes much laughter.

---

die to want die if I lack it

trifling prattling, playing with words

maid virgin or servant

fellow bedfellow, wife, companion or social equal

mistress woman who has command over a man's heart

thus humble (Ferdinand kneels or makes a low bow to her)

As bondage e'er of freedom as ever a prisoner greeted freedom

A thousand thousand a million farewells

surprised taken unawares or amazed

appertaining relating to this

butt is out barrel is empty

bear up, and board 'em drink up (sailors' toast, like 'cheers')

be brained like us have brains in the drunken condition of ours

totters is about to collapse

MIRANDA	At mine unworthiness, that dare not offer
	What I desire to give, and much less take 80
	What I shall die to want. But this is trifling,
	And all the more it seeks to hide itself
	The bigger bulk it shows. Hence, bashful cunning,
	And prompt me, plain and holy innocence.
	I am your wife, if you will marry me; 85
	If not, I'll die your maid. To be your fellow
	You may deny me, but I'll be your servant
	Whether you will or no.
FERDINAND	[*Kneeling*] My mistress, dearest,
	And I thus humble ever.
MIRANDA	My husband then?
FERDINAND	Aye, with a heart as willing 90
	As bondage e'er of freedom. Here's my hand.
MIRANDA	And mine, with my heart in't; and now farewell
	Till half an hour hence.
FERDINAND	A thousand thousand.
	Exeunt [*Ferdinand and Miranda separately*]
PROSPERO	So glad of this as they I cannot be,
	Who are surprised with all; but my rejoicing 95
	At nothing can be more. I'll to my book,
	For yet ere supper-time must I perform
	Much business appertaining. *Exit*

Act 3 Scene 2
Near Caliban's cave

Enter CALIBAN, STEPHANO *and* TRINCULO

STEPHANO   Tell not me. When the butt is out we will drink water, not
a drop before; therefore bear up, and board 'em. Servant monster,
drink to me.

TRINCULO   [*Aside*] Servant monster? The folly of this island! They say
there's but five upon this isle; we are three of them – if th'other   5
two be brained like us, the state totters.

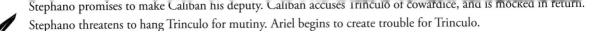

Stagecraft

A new master for Caliban (by yourself)

In some performances, Trinculo does not seem to be fully part of the conversation between Stephano and Caliban. His words are mostly directed to the audience until he is drawn into the quarrel at line 23. In contrast, in other performances he argues directly with Stephano.

- In your Director's Journal, make notes advising the actors on how to portray the three characters in the script opposite. How would you depict Trinculo in particular?

1 Trinculo – drunk, but perceptive

Trinculo is drunk, but he sees the foolishness of his companions. He ridicules them each time he speaks in lines 4–28 and uses puns, a language device characteristic of the court jester.

- Find each of Trinculo's puns and explain how it provides cues for comic stage business (see lines 9, 17 and 26).

- Suggest a gesture that Stephano might make to accompany his words when he threatens to hang Trinculo on 'the next tree' (line 31).

set (line 8) drunkenly fixed, staring

set (line 9) placed

brave splendid (ironic)

five and thirty leagues over a hundred miles

off and on one way or another or by fits and starts

standard standard-bearer (or able to stand)

list like, or keel over like a sinking ship

no standard reeling and drunk

run take flight

go walk

lie lie down, or tell lies

in case ready (brave enough)

deboshed drunken, lecherous

monstrous lie enormous untruth and also a lie told by a monster

quoth he he says

natural idiot, simpleton

keep … tongue in your head speak civilly

the next tree I will hang you from the next tree

subject servant

suit proposition, request

Marry by St Mary (an oath)

cunning knowledge or trickery

valiant master (Stephano)

STEPHANO Drink, servant monster, when I bid thee; thy eyes are almost set in thy head.

TRINCULO Where should they be set else? He were a brave monster indeed if they were set in his tail. 10

STEPHANO My man-monster hath drowned his tongue in sack. For my part, the sea cannot drown me – I swam, ere I could recover the shore, five and thirty leagues off and on. By this light, thou shalt be my lieutenant, monster, or my standard.

TRINCULO Your lieutenant if you list; he's no standard. 15

STEPHANO We'll not run, monsieur monster.

TRINCULO Nor go neither; but you'll lie like dogs, and yet say nothing neither.

STEPHANO Moon-calf, speak once in thy life, if thou beest a good moon-calf. 20

CALIBAN How does thy honour? Let me lick thy shoe. I'll not serve him, he is not valiant.

TRINCULO Thou liest, most ignorant monster; I am in case to jostle a constable. Why, thou deboshed fish thou, was there ever man a coward that hath drunk so much sack as I today? Wilt thou tell 25 a monstrous lie, being but half a fish, and half a monster?

CALIBAN Lo, how he mocks me. Wilt thou let him, my lord?

TRINCULO 'Lord', quoth he? That a monster should be such a natural!

CALIBAN Lo, lo again! Bite him to death, I prithee.

STEPHANO Trinculo, keep a good tongue in your head. If you prove a 30 mutineer, the next tree. The poor monster's my subject, and he shall not suffer indignity.

CALIBAN I thank my noble lord. Wilt thou be pleased to hearken once again to the suit I made to thee?

STEPHANO Marry will I. Kneel, and repeat it. I will stand, and so shall 35 Trinculo.

Enter ARIEL *invisible*

CALIBAN As I told thee before, I am subject to a tyrant, a sorcerer, that by his cunning hath cheated me of the island.

ARIEL Thou liest.

CALIBAN [*To Trinculo*] Thou liest, thou jesting monkey thou. I would 40 my valiant master would destroy thee. I do not lie.

Themes

Comic echoes of usurpation (by yourself)

The three drunkards provide a comic parody of one of the main themes of the play: usurpation (the overthrow of a rightful ruler). Stephano tries to behave like a king, and demands that his subjects obey him. He has already threatened Trinculo with hanging ('the next tree'). Caliban's plot to overthrow Prospero is a comic reflection of the way in which Antonio seized the throne of Milan from Prospero, and of the courtiers' conspiracy to kill Alonso. Even Stephano's threat to Trinculo, 'I will supplant some of your teeth' (line 43), echoes the theme ('supplant' literally means uproot).

• Write a paragraph on how this theme has developed in the play so far, and how it links these two strands of the plot. Remember to use embedded quotations to support your ideas.

Stagecraft

Comedy and slapstick

a Trinculo gets a beating for something he hasn't done. Stephano thinks Trinculo is mocking him, but Ariel is really to blame, getting Trinculo into trouble by echoing his earlier accusation at line 23 and imitating his voice at lines 39, 56 and 67.

• Work out how Ariel moves, how close he stands to Trinculo and how he behaves after he has spoken. In some performances Trinculo reacts with astonishment to Ariel's words; in others he is bemused by the accusations from the others, which suggests that he does not hear Ariel.

b Already imagining that he is king of the island, Stephano strikes Trinculo at line 68. Trinculo blames his beating on drink ('This can sack and drinking do' means 'This is what wine makes you do'). In some productions Trinculo speaks angrily, in others sulkily, in others fearfully, afraid of another beating.

• Practise speaking Trinculo's lines in the script opposite in different tones and to draw different reactions from an audience. Devise suitable slapstick for this part of the scene, and experiment with pulling off boots, or playing with hats or chairs.

Mum then hush

this thing (Trinculo)

compassed brought about
party person concerned

pied ninny many-coloured fool
patch jester's costume

brine salt water
quick freshes flowing springs of fresh water

stockfish dried, salted cod (softened by beating)

give me the lie call me a liar

pox curse
murrain plague
devil take your fingers (Trinculo curses the hand that just struck him)

STEPHANO Trinculo, if you trouble him any more in's tale, by this
hand, I will supplant some of your teeth.

TRINCULO Why, I said nothing.

STEPHANO Mum then, and no more. [*To Caliban*] Proceed.   45

CALIBAN I say by sorcery he got this isle;
From me he got it. If thy greatness will
Revenge it on him – for I know thou dar'st,
But this thing dare not –

STEPHANO That's most certain.   50

CALIBAN Thou shalt be lord of it, and I'll serve thee.

STEPHANO How now shall this be compassed? Canst thou bring me to
the party?

CALIBAN Yea, yea, my lord, I'll yield him thee asleep,
Where thou mayst knock a nail into his head.   55

ARIEL Thou liest, thou canst not.

CALIBAN What a pied ninny's this? [*To Trinculo*] Thou scurvy patch!
[*To Stephano*] I do beseech thy greatness give him blows,
And take his bottle from him. When that's gone,
He shall drink nought but brine, for I'll not show him   60
Where the quick freshes are.

STEPHANO Trinculo, run into no further danger. Interrupt the monster
one word further, and by this hand, I'll turn my mercy out o'doors,
and make a stockfish of thee.

TRINCULO Why, what did I? I did nothing. I'll go farther off.   65

STEPHANO Didst thou not say he lied?

ARIEL Thou liest.

STEPHANO Do I so?

[*Strikes Trinculo*]

Take thou that! As you like this, give me the lie another time.

TRINCULO I did not give the lie. Out o'your wits, and hearing too? A   70
pox o'your bottle! This can sack and drinking do. A murrain on
your monster, and the devil take your fingers!

CALIBAN Ha, ha, ha!

STEPHANO Now forward with your tale. [*To Trinculo*] Prithee stand
further off.   75

CALIBAN Beat him enough; after a little time
I'll beat him too.

Caliban proposes a plan to kill Prospero. Stephano agrees to do the deed. He says that he will take Miranda as his queen, and will make Trinculo and Caliban his deputies. Stephano apologises for beating Trinculo.

Characters

Caliban's plot (in pairs)

Caliban urges Stephano to burn the books that give Prospero his magical powers. (The same books probably led to Prospero's overthrow as duke of Milan, because he was so busy studying them that he neglected state affairs.) Caliban also claims that Prospero's spirits loathe their master: 'they all do hate him / As rootedly as I.'

*   Experiment with different ways of speaking Caliban's lines 79–95 to reveal his character at this point in the play. Try packing them with anger and resentment – and persuasive power.

paunch him stab him in the stomach

wezand windpipe, throat

sot drunkard, fool

rootedly firmly

brave ùtensils household goods

deck decorate

nonpareil without equal in beauty

1 'Ex-cell-ent' – is it sarcasm?

In the 1993 Royal Shakespeare Company (RSC) production of *The Tempest*, Trinculo stretched out his one word in line 102 very slowly and sarcastically: 'Ex-cell-ent'. In other productions, he adopts a sulky tone that prompts Stephano to try to make amends.

*   How would you advise Trinculo to speak this one word? Why?

become thy bed suit your bed

brave brood many children

2 Contrasting episodes

Lines 96–101 make a stark contrast with the tender love scene between Ferdinand and Miranda. Some of the comedy is shown in the photograph below, as the very drunk Trinculo and Stephano offer Caliban alcohol, while Ariel looks on.

*   Write a paragraph to explain the effect you would try to create with these lines if you were directing the play. What reaction would you want from your audience?

'save our graces God save us

viceroys deputies to the king

jocund happy

troll the catch sing the song loudly and in rounds (where each singer takes up the same tune in sequence)

but whilere just now

STEPHANO	Stand farther. [*To Caliban*] Come, proceed.
CALIBAN	Why, as I told thee, 'tis a custom with him
	I'th'afternoon to sleep. There thou mayst brain him,
	Having first seized his books; or with a log
	Batter his skull, or paunch him with a stake,
	Or cut his wezand with thy knife. Remember
	First to possess his books; for without them
	He's but a sot, as I am, nor hath not
	One spirit to command – they all do hate him
	As rootedly as I. Burn but his books;
	He has brave ùtensils – for so he calls them –
	Which when he has a house, he'll deck withal.
	And that most deeply to consider, is
	The beauty of his daughter. He himself
	Calls her a nonpareil. I never saw a woman
	But only Sycorax my dam, and she;
	But she as far surpasseth Sycorax
	As great'st does least.
STEPHANO	Is it so brave a lass?
CALIBAN	Ay, lord, she will become thy bed, I warrant,
	And bring thee forth brave brood.
STEPHANO	Monster, I will kill this man. His daughter and I will be king and queen – 'save our graces! – and Trinculo and thyself shall be viceroys. Dost thou like the plot, Trinculo?
TRINCULO	Excellent.
STEPHANO	Give me thy hand. I am sorry I beat thee. But while thou liv'st, keep a good tongue in thy head.
CALIBAN	Within this half hour will he be asleep,
	Wilt thou destroy him then?
STEPHANO	Ay, on mine honour.
ARIEL	This will I tell my master.
CALIBAN	Thou mak'st me merry. I am full of pleasure,
	Let us be jocund. Will you troll the catch
	You taught me but whilere?

80

85

90

95

100

105

110

The three drunkards sing raucously, but Ariel's music strikes fear into Stephano and Trinculo. Caliban urges them not to be afraid, and describes delightful sounds and wonderful dreams. They follow Ariel's music.

1 Caliban's dream (in small groups)

Stephano and Trinculo are terror-stricken by Ariel's music. But Caliban tells them about the delightful noises of the island and his wonderful dreams. His lines 127–35 are among the best known and most haunting of Shakespeare's verse. Try the following activities to experience the quality of the poetry.

a **Choral speaking** Devise a way of speaking the lines so that everyone in the group shares them. Use echoes and repetitions.

b **Different emotional tones** Explore ways of speaking the lines in different tones of voice, such as full of wonder and awe, sadly, and/or with musical accompaniment.

c **Accompanying gestures** Work out an action or gesture for one key word or image in each line.

Write about it

Poetry and prose

As a general rule in Shakespeare's plays, high-status characters speak in verse (poetry), and comic or low-status characters speak in prose. In lines 127–35, the low-status Caliban speaks some of Shakespeare's greatest poetry. These poignant and memorable lines are delivered by a character whom the others call 'monster'. Does this show another side to Caliban? What effects on the audience do these lines have?

• Write one or two paragraphs to answer these questions, referring closely to this part of the script by using embedded quotations. In particular, you should explore the ideas of nature and nurture that are among the play's thematic concerns. Consider also the language features Shakespeare uses to create his effects (look for metaphors, alliteration, onomatopoeia and repetition of words or ideas).

do reason do anything reasonable

Flout 'em, and scout 'em mock them and jeer at them

tabor drum

Nobody the invisible man
thou beest you are
list wish, please

airs tunes
twangling instruments (plucked string instruments such as the lute or harp)
hum make a continuous noise

by and by soon

lays it on plays the drum splendidly

STEPHANO   At thy request, monster, I will do reason, any reason. Come
on, Trinculo, let us sing.
[*They sing*] Flout 'em, and scout 'em
      And scout 'em, and flout 'em.   115
            Thought is free.

CALIBAN   That's not the tune.

Ariel plays the tune on a tabor and pipe

STEPHANO   What is this same?

TRINCULO   This is the tune of our catch, played by the picture of
Nobody.   120

STEPHANO   If thou beest a man, show thyself in thy likeness: if thou
beest a devil, take't as thou list.

TRINCULO   O, forgive me my sins!

STEPHANO   He that dies pays all debts! I defy thee! Mercy upon us!

CALIBAN   Art thou afeared?   125

STEPHANO   No, monster, not I.

CALIBAN   Be not afeared; the isle is full of noises,
      Sounds, and sweet airs, that give delight and hurt not.
      Sometimes a thousand twangling instruments
      Will hum about mine ears; and sometime voices,   130
      That if I then had waked after long sleep,
      Will make me sleep again; and then in dreaming,
      The clouds methought would open, and show riches
      Ready to drop upon me, that when I waked
      I cried to dream again.   135

STEPHANO   This will prove a brave kingdom to me, where I shall have
my music for nothing.

CALIBAN   When Prospero is destroyed.

STEPHANO   That shall be by and by: I remember the story.

[*Exit Ariel, playing music*]

TRINCULO   The sound is going away; let's follow it, and after do our   140
work.

STEPHANO   Lead, monster, we'll follow. I would I could see this taborer,
he lays it on.

TRINCULO   [*To Caliban*] Wilt come? I'll follow Stephano.

Exeunt

Gonzalo and Alonso are wearied by their wanderings. Alonso gives up hope of finding Ferdinand alive. Sebastian and Antonio again plot to murder Alonso. A banquet magically appears, brought in by Prospero's spirits.

Themes

A moral maze and spiritual journey

Some critics argue that lines 2–3 symbolise the spiritual journey of King Alonso. He is wandering in a labyrinth ('maze'), unable to find his way out. As you read on, keep in mind the idea of Alonso travelling on a symbolic journey where he learns, through suffering, to repent of his wrong-doings. During this time, Antonio and Sebastian remain unchanged – and once again they plan to murder Alonso.

a Suggest how lines 11–17 could be played to emphasise the contrast between the villainy of Antonio and Sebastian, and the vulnerability of Alonso and Gonzalo.

b Describe how the idea of a moral journey – where a person develops morally and spiritually through experience and suffering – helps you understand each of the characters in this scene. What do you predict will happen next?

1 Responding to stage directions (in small groups)

a Every production tries to present the stage directions following lines 17 and 19 as dramatically and imaginatively as possible. The stage directions are an exciting opportunity for you to exercise your imagination. Discuss your response to each of the following:

- *'Solemn and strange music'* Compose your own music or find some music that might fit this stage direction.
- 'PROSPERO *on the top'* How could this be shown?
- *'invisible'* How would you suggest Prospero's invisibility?
- *'Enter several strange shapes'* Costumes? Appearance?
- *'bringing in a banquet'* How?
- *'dance about it'* How might they dance to the music you created above?
- *'with gentle actions of salutations'* How do they salute the king?
- *'inviting the king, etc. to eat'* With what gestures and movements?
- *'they depart'* Devise a dramatic departure.

b How would you want a set designer, costume designer, composer and sound-effects team to portray the spirits in the most effective way? Try to capture the wonder, mystery and fear that these shapes would inspire, as well as describing how the stage would be set.

By'r lakin by our Lady (the Virgin Mary)

forth-rights and meanders straight and winding paths

By your patience with your permission

attached seized

To th'dulling of my spirits that makes me feel hopelessness

put off abandon

frustrate vain, defeated

for one repulse because of our first failure

purpose murder

advantage opportunity

throughly thoroughly, perfectly

travail travel-weariness

Act 3 Scene 3
A remote part of the island

Enter ALONSO, SEBASTIAN, ANTONIO, GONZALO, ADRIAN,
FRANCISCO *and others*

GONZALO   By'r lakin, I can go no further, sir,
My old bones aches. Here's a maze trod indeed
Through forth-rights and meanders. By your patience,
I needs must rest me.

ALONSO   Old lord, I cannot blame thee,
Who am myself attached with weariness   5
To th'dulling of my spirits. Sit down, and rest.
Even here I will put off my hope, and keep it
No longer for my flatterer. He is drowned
Whom thus we stray to find, and the sea mocks
Our frustrate search on land. Well, let him go.   10

ANTONIO   [*Drawing Sebastian aside*] I am right glad that he's so out of hope.
Do not for one repulse forgo the purpose
That you resolved t'effect.

SEBASTIAN   [*To Antonio*]   The next advantage
Will we take throughly.

ANTONIO   Let it be tonight;
For now they are oppressed with travail, they   15
Will not, nor cannot use such vigilance
As when they're fresh.

SEBASTIAN   I say tonight: no more.

Solemn and strange music, and [*enter*] PROSPERO *on the top, invisible*

ALONSO   What harmony is this? my good friends, hark!
GONZALO   Marvellous sweet music.

*Enter several strange shapes, bringing in a banquet, and dance about it
with gentle actions of salutations, and inviting the king, etc. to eat, they
depart*

The courtiers wonder at what they have seen, saying it resembled something from mythology or travellers' tales. Prospero comments on the evil of Alonso, Sebastian and Antonio, and hints at further marvels.

1 Fantastic animals, birds – and tales (in pairs)

Lines 20–49 are rich in echoes of the fantasies of fable and mythology, and the travellers' tales that the early explorers brought home to Shakespeare's England:

- **'unicorns'** (line 22) Mythical horses with a long, spiked horn.
- **'phoenix'** (lines 23–4) A fabulous bird., only one of which lived at any time. It burned itself upon a funeral pyre ('throne'), and arose, new-born, from the ashes.
- **'Travellers ne'er did lie'** (lines 26–7) Explorers brought back incredible stories of what they had seen in distant lands. Their fantastic tales were often ridiculed.

a Imagine the characters in this scene are back safely in Milan and are describing what it was like to be on the island, seeing the food and the spirits, and experiencing the magic, the fear, the sadness and the wonder. Do they stick to the truth of the story or do they embellish it with more extravagant accounts of their adventures on the island and the creatures they met there? Discuss this in your pairs.

b In role as one of the characters in the script opposite, tell the story to your partner, or write a diary entry for that character in which they reflect on these events.

Write about it

You should have been there …

Almost every line in the script opposite (except Prospero's) contains an expression of wonder or disbelief.

- Write down a word or phrase in each line that the actor could emphasise to express a sense of wonder.
- Use these words to create a few headlines for two newspapers – a tabloid and a broadsheet – that are both featuring the story of the travellers' experiences on the island.

---

kind keepers guardian angels
living drollery comic or puppet show

want credit lack credibility

certes certainly

human generation humankind

muse marvel at

Praise in departing there's more to come (keep your praise till the end)

viands food
stomachs appetites
Dewlapped like bulls (a dewlap is the flap of skin hanging from the throats of cows and other animals)
such men (travellers reported that they had seen men whose heads were in their chests – see also 'The Anthropophagi' in *Othello*, Act 1 Scene 3, lines 143–4)
Each … for one (explorers could finance their expeditions by betting on their chances of success; they deposited a sum of money before they left and if they returned safely, they could claim five times that)
Good warrant of secure proof

ALONSO	Give us kind keepers, heavens! What were these?	20
SEBASTIAN	A living drollery! Now I will believe	
	That there are unicorns; that in Arabia	
	There is one tree, the phoenix' throne, one phoenix	
	At this hour reigning there.	
ANTONIO	I'll believe both;	
	And what does else want credit, come to me	25
	And I'll be sworn 'tis true. Travellers ne'er did lie,	
	Though fools at home condemn 'em.	
GONZALO	If in Naples	
	I should report this now, would they believe me?	
	If I should say I saw such islanders –	
	For certes, these are people of the island –	30
	Who though they are of monstrous shape, yet note	
	Their manners are more gentle, kind, than of	
	Our human generation you shall find	
	Many, nay almost any.	
PROSPERO	[*Aside*] Honest lord,	
	Thou hast said well – for some of you there present	35
	Are worse than devils.	
ALONSO	I cannot too much muse,	
	Such shapes, such gesture, and such sound, expressing –	
	Although they want the use of tongue – a kind	
	Of excellent dumb discourse.	
PROSPERO	[*Aside*] Praise in departing.	
FRANCISCO	They vanished strangely.	
SEBASTIAN	No matter, since they	40
	Have left their viands behind; for we have stomachs.	
	Wilt please you taste of what is here?	
ALONSO	Not I.	
GONZALO	Faith, sir, you need not fear. When we were boys,	
	Who would believe that there were mountaineers,	
	Dewlapped like bulls, whose throats had hanging at 'em	45
	Wallets of flesh? Or that there were such men	
	Whose heads stood in their breasts? Which now we find	
	Each putter-out of five for one will bring us	
	Good warrant of.	

stand to begin eating

harpy monster in Greek mythology with the head and torso of a woman, and the tail, wings and talons of a bird

to instrument control over

this lower world Earth

never-surfeited ever hungry, never satisfied

you ... unfit to live because of your sin you do not deserve human company

suchlike valour bravery of insane men that leads to desperate acts

Their proper selves themselves

tempered made hard

still-closing that always close up again

dowl tiny feather

plume plumage

fellow ministers spirits

massy heavy

business purpose

requit it repaid the crime of abandoning Prospero and Miranda to the sea

powers divine rulers

creatures natural creation

bereft robbed, deprived

Ling'ring perdition slow ruin and destruction

any death ... once any immediate death sentence

is nothing but there is no alternative

heart's sorrow repentance, grief

clear life ensuing future life free from immorality

Themes

'You are three men of sin'

After accusing the 'men of sin', Ariel declares them 'unfit to live'. He reminds them of their powerlessness, of their overthrow of Prospero, and of the ruin they now face as a result. Ariel tells them that only sorrowful repentance and virtuous living can save them now ('heart's sorrow, / And a clear life ensuing').

* Practise ways of speaking Ariel's lines for the greatest dramatic effect. Remember, this speech is in iambic pentameter, so listen out for the underlying rhythmical sound of the verse.

Characters

Internal monologues (in small groups)

The notion that God's justice would ultimately prevail was pervasive in Shakespeare's day. It was referred to in legal proceedings and in religious sermons and pamphlets.

* Script an internal monologue for each of the characters as they hear what the harpy (Ariel) says to them. What are they thinking and feeling? Are they sorry, or are they hard-hearted and full of excuses?

ALONSO   I will stand to, and feed,
          Although my last, no matter, since I feel   50
          The best is past. Brother, my lord the duke,
          Stand to and do as we.

          Thunder and lightning. Enter ARIEL, *like a harpy, claps his wings upon*
              the table, and with a quaint device the banquet vanishes

ARIEL   You are three men of sin, whom Destiny –
          That hath to instrument this lower world,
          And what is in't – the never-surfeited sea   55
          Hath caused to belch up you. And on this island,
          Where man doth not inhabit – you 'mongst men
          Being most unfit to live – I have made you mad;
          And even with suchlike valour men hang and drown
          Their proper selves.
                    [*Alonso, Sebastian, Antonio draw their swords*]
                              You fools! I and my fellows   60
          Are ministers of Fate. The elements
          Of whom your swords are tempered may as well
          Wound the loud winds, or with bemocked-at stabs
          Kill the still-closing waters, as diminish
          One dowl that's in my plume. My fellow ministers   65
          Are like invulnerable. If you could hurt,
          Your swords are now too massy for your strengths,
          And will not be uplifted. But remember –
          For that's my business to you – that you three
          From Milan did supplant good Prospero;   70
          Exposed unto the sea – which hath requit it –
          Him, and his innocent child; for which foul deed,
          The powers, delaying, not forgetting, have
          Incensed the seas and shores, yea, all the creatures
          Against your peace. Thee of thy son, Alonso,   75
          They have bereft; and do pronounce by me
          Ling'ring perdition – worse than any death
          Can be at once – shall step by step attend
          You, and your ways; whose wraths to guard you from –
          Which here, in this most desolate isle, else falls   80
          Upon your heads – is nothing but heart's sorrow,
          And a clear life ensuing.

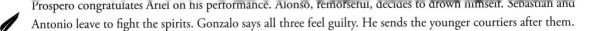
1 A splendid performance (in small groups)

Prospero is delighted with how Ariel has played his part ('Bravely': excellently). His other spirit servants have also put on a splendid spectacle ('with good life / And observation strange': vividly and imaginatively). Just what did the 'shapes' (spirits) do in support of Ariel?

- Form a discussion group for the actors playing Prospero's spirit servants. With the director in charge, discuss what movements and facial expressions might work best in this presentation to Alonso, Sebastian and Antonio. It seems that each spirit does something different, using its particular talents ('several kinds').

Write about it

Poison and hidden sin (in pairs)

Prospero's plan is working. Gonzalo sees the frenzy of the three men as a long-awaited consequence of their sin, echoing Ariel's message about delayed justice. He uses the **simile** (see p. 166) of slow-working poison to describe the way that their sins are now affecting them.

    This part of the play also draws from the belief that sinfulness will always torment those who do not repent. In his guilt, Alonso feels accused by Nature and he experiences a great sense of remorse for wronging Prospero. He believes he has been punished for this by the death of his son Ferdinand, and decides that death by drowning must also be his destiny.

- Discuss how the imagery in the script opposite helps us to understand what Alonso is feeling. Then write one or two paragraphs to describe Alonso's guilt and to explore the effect of the language Gonzalo uses when he sees Alonso's despair.

2 Do Antonio and Sebastian feel guilt? (in pairs)

Sebastian and Antonio are determined to resist. They make no clear expression of guilt, showing only a desire to fight.

a Talk together about whether you think Sebastian and Antonio should show any acknowledgement of guilt. If so, how (for example, by leaving a long pause before speaking 'But one fiend at a time').

b Write a paragraph explaining whether you think Sebastian and Antonio feel any guilt. Use quotations from the script and consider Gonzalo's and Alonso's responses as well as Sebastian's and Antonio's words.

---

mocks and mows insulting gestures and faces

figure part

devouring completely

bated omitted

So in the same way

good life with great liveliness or a lifelike performance

observation strange amazingly observant care

meaner ministers lesser spirits

several kinds distinct, separate roles

distractions mental conflicts or disturbances

fits paroxysms

dreadful frightening

bass my trespass loudly sing my wrong-doing

Therefore for that

i'th'ooze is bedded lies in the mud of the sea-bed

plummet sounded plumb-line measured

second supporter, assistant

desperate despairing

'gins begins

of suppler joints younger

ecstasy madness

He vanishes in thunder; then, to soft music, enter the shapes again, and
dance, with mocks and mows, and [then depart] carrying out the table

PROSPERO Bravely the figure of this harpy hast thou
Performed, my Ariel; a grace it had devouring.
Of my instruction hast thou nothing bated   85
In what thou hadst to say. So, with good life
And observation strange, my meaner ministers
Their several kinds have done. My high charms work,
And these, mine enemies, are all knit up
In their distractions. They now are in my power;   90
And in these fits I leave them, while I visit
Young Ferdinand, whom they suppose is drowned,
And his and mine loved darling.   [*Exit*]

GONZALO I'th'name of something holy, sir, why stand you
In this strange stare?

ALONSO   O, it is monstrous: monstrous!   95
Methought the billows spoke and told me of it,
The winds did sing it to me, and the thunder,
That deep and dreadful organ-pipe, pronounced
The name of Prosper. It did bass my trespass;
Therefore my son i'th'ooze is bedded; and   100
I'll seek him deeper than e'er plummet sounded,
And with him there lie mudded.   *Exit*

SEBASTIAN But one fiend at a time, I'll fight their legions o'er.
ANTONIO I'll be thy second.

                              Exeunt [Sebastian and Antonio]

GONZALO All three of them are desperate. Their great guilt,   105
Like poison given to work a great time after,
Now 'gins to bite the spirits. I do beseech you,
That are of suppler joints, follow them swiftly,
And hinder them from what this ecstasy
May now provoke them to.

ADRIAN   Follow, I pray you.   110

                              Exeunt

Looking back at Act 3
Activities for groups or individuals

1 Spectacle and drama

Act 3 ends very dramatically. There is the spectacle of Ariel's fellow spirits, who appear as 'strange shapes' and dance, make 'gentle actions of salutations', pull faces ('mocks and mows') and set out a banquet for the courtiers. There is also the description of imagined creatures and spectacular discoveries during voyages of exploration. In addition, there is the drama of Ariel's appearance as a harpy, the frenzied reaction of the 'three men of sin' and their hurried exit off the stage.

- In role as a director, imagine you are having a conversation with a theatre critic. Describe how you would stage the ending of this act. Consider how you would link spectacle and drama with the main themes of the play.
- Script the conversation between these two people. Make sure the theatre critic asks the director some interesting questions about costume, stage design, special effects and the impact on the audience.

2 Three scenes, three minutes

Devise a mini version of Act 3, expressing the essence of each scene in one minute. To prepare, read through the summaries at the top of each left-hand page in Act 3.

3 Different views of the island

a Write a sentence that begins: 'I see this island as …' for each of the following characters at this point in the play: Prospero, Miranda, Caliban, Ariel, Alonso, Antonio, Ferdinand, Stephano, Trinculo, Gonzalo.

b Choose two characters and create a past for them, which fills in the gaps of our knowledge of them so far. Write a first-person account of what their life may have been like. Your aim is to imaginatively re-create their past in order to understand their present behaviour and motivations.

4 Thematic focus

a Look back at the 'Themes' boxes in this act. In small groups, talk about these themes. Draw a chart to show how they interrelate, and support your chart with quotations and examples. Remember that the following themes are linked: the relationship between appearance and reality, illusion and magic, imprisonment and freedom, and how selfishness and ambition relate to authority and power.

b Present a case to the rest of the class. What is the most important single theme? What are the most important combinations of themes? Why did you reach these conclusions? If you were staging a production of the play, which themes would you highlight, and what elements of stagecraft would you employ to emphasise them?

5 Control and surveillance

Prospero's control and Ariel's surveillance link all three plot strands in the play (Miranda and Ferdinand; Caliban and the drunken servants; Alonso and the courtiers).

- List all the examples of Prospero's control and Ariel's surveillance in Act 3. Considering what you know about their plots, write out a detailed prediction for what might happen in the next act. Do you think that Prospero will have his enemies killed? Will he enchant them further? Or will he forgive them?
- As you write, consider what you know about the characters so far. Also, think about the genre of the play and conduct further research into the characteristics of a romance play. Justify your predictions about Act 4 by explaining your reasons with reference to quotations and examples from the first three acts of the play.

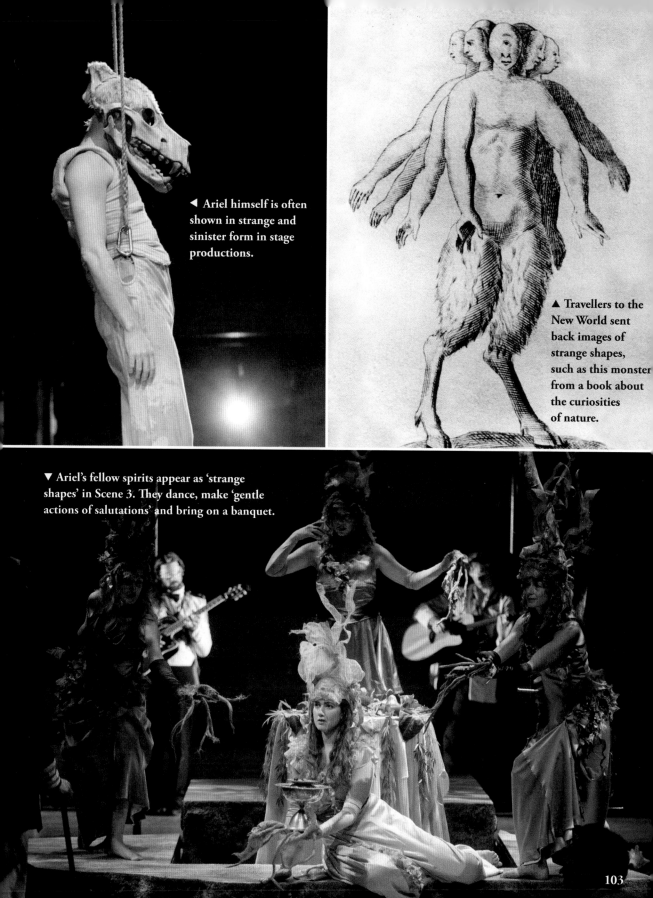

◀ Ariel himself is often shown in strange and sinister form in stage productions.

▲ Travellers to the New World sent back images of strange shapes, such as this monster from a book about the curiosities of nature.

▼ Ariel's fellow spirits appear as 'strange shapes' in Scene 3. They dance, make 'gentle actions of salutations' and bring on a banquet.

103

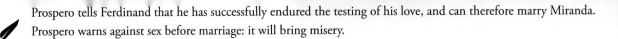

Prospero tells Ferdinand that he has successfully endured the testing of his love, and can therefore marry Miranda. Prospero warns against sex before marriage: it will bring misery.

Characters

Prospero: simple pride or greedy ownership? (in pairs)

Act 4 begins with two complex speeches by Prospero. In lines 1–11, he tells Ferdinand that he has proven his love for Miranda, and he gives the couple his blessing as a reward.

a Read Prospero's words carefully. Do you think he is being over-protective ('that for which I live'), or are his words completely understandable given the circumstances? Why does he refer to her as 'one third of [his] life'? Discuss this with your partner. Remember that in Shakespeare's day, a girl was considered to be her father's property until she was married.

b Talk together about how Prospero's speeches opposite add to our understanding of this character. Write down your conclusions to help you with the next activity.

Write about it

Act convincingly

In lines 14–22 (from 'But'), Prospero warns Ferdinand not to have sexual intercourse with Miranda before they marry. If he does, says Prospero, discord and hatred will follow. He repeats the warning later, in lines 51–4.

Many people think that Prospero's words show that *The Tempest* was specially performed at the wedding celebrations in 1612–13 of Princess Elizabeth, daughter of King James. At the time, there was a strong belief that premarital sex was undesirable (although many women – including Shakespeare's wife – were pregnant on their wedding day).

• Imagine that you are directing *The Tempest*. The actor playing Prospero writes you a private note: 'I'm having real problems with how to deliver this speech. It doesn't feel right just to play Prospero as such a strict father here, but his words are pretty harsh. I wonder what is motivating him to talk like this. Will you write a paragraph or two to help me, please?' Write your reply.

austerely severely

punished you made you suffer

Your compensation ... amends your reward makes up for it

third ... life (Miranda)

tender to thy hand give you

thy vexations the physical trials

trials tests

strangely wonderfully

ratify confirm

boast her of boast of her

outstrip all praise exceed the best things that could be said of her

halt lag, limp

against an oracle even if a prophet denied it

purchased won

virgin-knot virginity, chastity

sanctimonious ceremonies sacred marriage rites

aspersion blessing (like rain on crops)

make this contract grow cause this marriage to produce children

loathly repulsive

Hymen Greek god of marriage (who carried a lamp)

Act 4 Scene 1
Near Prospero's cave

Enter PROSPERO, FERDINAND *and* MIRANDA

PROSPERO [*To Ferdinand*] If I have too austerely punished you
      Your compensation makes amends, for I
      Have given you here a third of mine own life,
      Or that for which I live; who once again
      I tender to thy hand. All thy vexations   5
      Were but my trials of thy love, and thou
      Hast strangely stood the test. Here, afore heaven,
      I ratify this my rich gift. O Ferdinand,
      Do not smile at me, that I boast her of,
      For thou shalt find she will outstrip all praise 10
      And make it halt behind her.
FERDINAND I do believe it against an oracle.
PROSPERO Then, as my gift, and thine own acquisition
      Worthily purchased, take my daughter. But
      If thou dost break her virgin-knot before   15
      All sanctimonious ceremonies may
      With full and holy rite be ministered,
      No sweet aspersion shall the heavens let fall
      To make this contract grow; but barren hate,
      Sour-eyed disdain and discord shall bestrew 20
      The union of your bed with weeds so loathly
      That you shall hate it both. Therefore take heed,
      As Hymen's lamps shall light you.

Stagecraft

Ariel: a surrogate child? (in small groups)

The relationship between Prospero and Ariel is a fascinating one. Are they simply master and servant, or something more complex? Has Ariel observed Miranda's growing independence and moved in to take her place as Prospero's surrogate child? Think about how Prospero and Ariel might feel towards each other by this stage of the play.

- Discuss how line 48 ('Do you love me master? No?') should be spoken: sadly, fearfully, playfully, or in some other manner?
- Decide how Prospero should speak his reply in line 49 ('Dearly, my delicate Ariel.')

1 A second warning (in pairs)

In lines 51–2, Prospero speaks again to Ferdinand about his conduct towards Miranda, telling him to keep his desires in check ('Do not give dalliance / Too much the rein').

a Talk together about whether you think something in Prospero's character provokes this second warning, or whether Ferdinand and Miranda are giving 'dalliance the rein' (perhaps behaving too intimately too soon). Which seems more likely?

b Imagine that you are a counsellor advising Miranda and Ferdinand on their relationship. Write a short letter to both of them outlining what you think are the key issues and how they might be resolved.

▼ In the 2010 film adaptation of *The Tempest*, Prospero became Prospera and was played by a woman. The director explored the complex relationship between this character and Ariel (played by a man), asking the audience to think about gender, age and emotional attachments.

---

fair issue beautiful children

With such love … now if this love continues with this intensity

murkiest den darkest hiding place

oppòrtune appropriate (for seduction)

suggestion temptation

worser genius bad angel

edge keenness of appetite

that day the wedding day

When I shall … below when the sun god's horses have stopped (Ferdinand says that on his wedding day time will seem to slow down)

foundered gone lame

potent powerful

meaner fellows fellow spirits

last service (the disappearing banquet)

the rabble fellow spirits

Some vanity of mine art a magical illusion

Presently? immediately?

twink the wink of an eye

mop and mow gestures and grimaces

conceive understand

true honourable

dalliance flirtatious behaviour

good night your vow you can say goodbye to your promise

FERDINAND	As I hope
	For quiet days, fair issue, and long life,
	With such love as 'tis now, the murkiest den, 25
	The most oppòrtune place, the strong'st suggestion
	Our worser genius can, shall never melt
	Mine honour into lust, to take away
	The edge of that day's celebration,
	When I shall think or Phoebus' steeds are foundered, 30
	Or night kept chained below.
PROSPERO	Fairly spoke.
	Sit then, and talk with her, she is thine own.
	What, Ariel! My industrious servant Ariel!

Enter ARIEL

ARIEL	What would my potent master? Here I am.
PROSPERO	Thou and thy meaner fellows your last service 35
	Did worthily perform; and I must use you
	In such another trick. Go bring the rabble –
	O'er whom I give thee power – here, to this place.
	Incite them to quick motion, for I must
	Bestow upon the eyes of this young couple 40
	Some vanity of mine art. It is my promise,
	And they expect it from me.
ARIEL	Presently?
PROSPERO	Ay: with a twink.
ARIEL	Before you can say 'come' and 'go',
	And breathe twice, and cry 'so, so', 45
	Each one tripping on his toe,
	Will be here with mop and mow.
	Do you love me master? No?
PROSPERO	Dearly, my delicate Ariel. Do not approach
	Till thou dost hear me call.
ARIEL	Well; I conceive. *Exit* 50
PROSPERO	[*To Ferdinand*] Look thou be true! Do not give dalliance
	Too much the rein. The strongest oaths are straw
	To th'fire i'th'blood. Be more abstemious,
	Or else good night your vow.

Stagecraft

Making it spectacular (in threes)

Masques were spectacular court entertainments, rich in elaborate scenery and gorgeous costumes – much like big production musicals, or blockbuster movies of today. They involved music, poetry and dance, as well as visual effects. They also used complex stage machinery to create striking illusions.

The masque that Prospero has arranged to impress Ferdinand and Miranda symbolises two major themes of *The Tempest*:

- **Harmony after the storm** The appearance of Iris, goddess of the rainbow, expresses the peace that follows a tempest. Just as a rainbow appears after a storm, so Iris herself is an emblem of Prospero's plan to see Ferdinand and Miranda married. This union will reconcile Milan and Naples after many years of trouble. Notice the words that link Iris to the rainbow: 'watery arch', 'many-coloured', 'blue bow', 'Rich scarf'.

- **Bounty and fertility** Ceres, goddess of the harvest, symbolises the riches that will result from the wedding. In lines 60–9, Iris describes the fertile natural world over which Ceres reigns.

a Imagine you are the costume designer for a new stage production of the play. Sketch costumes for both Iris and Ceres. What would you want the costumes to convey to the other actors, and to the audience? Label and annotate your ideas in discussion with each other. This plan could make an eye-catching wall display.

b Together, write 100 words for the production's programme, in which you outline the symbolism of your designs to a reader. Keep a copy of this in your Director's Journal.

warrant promise

The white … liver the desires I feel for Miranda are moderated by her chastity

Well well said

a corollary one too many

want lack

pertly promptly

IRIS the rainbow

Ceres goddess of the earth and the harvest

leas pasture

vetches bean-producing plants

turfy covered with grass

meads meadows

stover hay

pionèd dug out

twillèd woven

spongy wet

hest command

betrims adorns

broom-groves gorse thickets, woods

dismissèd bachelor jilted lover

lass-lorn without a (female) lover

sea-marge sea-shore

dost air relax

queen o'th'sky Juno

amain speedily

saffron yellow

bosky acres woods

1 How do the characters respond?

The spectacle of the masque suddenly makes an audience of the other characters on stage, and Prospero becomes a director as well as a magician.

- If you were directing the play, where would you place the onstage audience at this point in the play? To what extent would you ask them to break down the 'fourth wall' and interact with the spirits? Write brief stage directions to each of the actors. Is Prospero proud of his work? Are the others impressed or afraid?

FERDINAND   I warrant you, sir,
   The white cold virgin snow upon my heart   55
   Abates the ardour of my liver.

PROSPERO   Well.
   Now come, my Ariel – bring a corollary,
   Rather than want a spirit; appear, and pertly.

      Soft music
   No tongue! All eyes! Be silent!

      Enter IRIS

IRIS   Ceres, most bounteous lady, thy rich leas   60
   Of wheat, rye, barley, vetches, oats and peas;
   Thy turfy mountains, where live nibbling sheep,
   And flat meads thatched with stover, them to keep;
   Thy banks with pionèd and twillèd brims,
   Which spongy April at thy hest betrims   65
   To make cold nymphs chaste crowns; and thy broom-groves,
   Whose shadow the dismissèd bachelor loves,
   Being lass-lorn; thy pole-clipped vineyard,
   And thy sea-marge, sterile and rocky-hard,
   Where thou thyself dost air: the queen o'th'sky,   70
   Whose watery arch and messenger am I,
   Bids thee leave these, and with her sovereign grace,
   Here on this grass-plot, in this very place
   To come and sport. Her peacocks fly amain.
   Approach, rich Ceres, her to entertain.   75

      Enter CERES

CERES   Hail, many-coloured messenger, that ne'er
   Dost disobey the wife of Jupiter;
   Who, with thy saffron wings, upon my flowers
   Diffusest honey drops, refreshing showers,
   And with each end of thy blue bow dost crown   80
   My bosky acres, and my unshrubbed down,
   Rich scarf to my proud earth. Why hath thy queen
   Summoned me hither, to this short-grazed green?

Iris tells Ceres that they are meeting to celebrate a wedding. She assures Ceres that Venus and Cupid will not be present, and that they have failed to bewitch Ferdinand and Miranda. Juno and Ceres sing a blessing.

1 Classical mythology – a presentation (in sevens)

Like most Jacobean entertainment, Prospero's masque draws heavily upon classical mythology.

a Using the Internet, or any other resources available to you, carry out some research into Jacobean masques. Find out what they consisted of and why they were so popular in Shakespeare's day. Using this research and the information on page 108, put together a presentation to deliver to the class.

b Allocate each member of your group a character from the masque in the script opposite (Ceres, Iris, Juno, Venus, Cupid, Hymen, Proserpine). Find out more about these figures from mythology, and suggest how each one has a particular symbolic significance in *The Tempest*.

c Stage your own performance of the masque.

estate bestow

Venus goddess of love
her son Cupid
dusky Dis Pluto, god of the underworld
blind boy Cupid (traditionally portrayed as blind)
scandalled improper
society company
her deity Venus
Cutting the clouds parting the clouds
Paphos town in Cyprus, centre of Venus worship
wanton charm wicked spell
no bed-right ... paid they will not have intercourse
Mars's hot minion Venus
returned turned back
waspish-headed son spiteful Cupid
be ... out behave like a boy rather than a god
gait walk
Go with me accompany me
issue children
Long continuance a long life

increasing (with children, with growing love)
foison abundant harvest
garners grain stores

IRIS	A contract of true love to celebrate,	
	And some donation freely to estate	85
	On the blest lovers.	
CERES	Tell me, heavenly bow,	
	If Venus or her son, as thou dost know,	
	Do now attend the queen? Since they did plot	
	The means that dusky Dis my daughter got,	
	Her and her blind boy's scandalled company	90
	I have forsworn.	
IRIS	Of her society	
	Be not afraid. I met her deity	
	Cutting the clouds towards Paphos, and her son	
	Dove-drawn with her. Here thought they to have done	
	Some wanton charm upon this man and maid,	95
	Whose vows are, that no bed-right shall be paid	
	Till Hymen's torch be lighted – but in vain.	
	Mars's hot minion is returned again;	
	Her waspish-headed son has broke his arrows,	
	Swears he will shoot no more, but play with sparrows,	100
	And be a boy right out.	

[JUNO *descends*]

	Highest queen of state,	
	Great Juno comes, I know her by her gait.	
JUNO	How does my bounteous sister? Go with me	
	To bless this twain, that they may prosperous be,	
	And honoured in their issue.	105
	[*Singing*] Honour, riches, marriage-blessing,	
	Long continuance, and increasing,	
	Hourly joys be still upon you,	
	Juno sings her blessings on you.	
[CERES]	[*Singing*] Earth's increase, and foison plenty,	110
	Barns and garners never empty,	
	Vines, with clust'ring bunches growing,	
	Plants, with goodly burden bowing;	
	Spring come to you at the farthest,	
	In the very end of harvest.	115
	Scarcity and want shall shun you,	
	Ceres' blessing so is on you.	

Prospero says that the spirits are enacting his fantasies. Ferdinand is full of happy wonder. Harvesters and nymphs dance at Iris's command, but are ordered off by Prospero when he remembers Caliban's plot.

Characters

Ferdinand: shallow, deep or deluded? (in small groups)

In lines 122–4, Ferdinand refers to the island as a 'paradise'. What does this say about him?

- Is he genuinely impressed by his surroundings and the events that have taken place since his arrival? Is he saying that having such a father, and a dutiful wife, are the most important things in a man's life? Or do you think he has fallen under Prospero's spell? Talk about your views of Ferdinand at this point in the play.

1 Choreographing a large cast

The arrival of 'certain reapers' and 'nymphs' means that the stage is suddenly very busy. This presents challenges for the whole cast.

- Imagine that you are in charge of choreography. Draw up a plan of the stage in which you give clear guidelines about where all the actors should be positioned, and when and how they should move. Make sure your design is clearly annotated.

Stagecraft

Making a mini-masque (in large groups)

a Bringing together all the work you have done on the masque, write out a version of Prospero's entertainment in modern prose. Make sure you stick closely to Shakespeare's meaning while still bringing the language up to date.

b Using your modern script, stage your own mini-masque for the rest of the class. Members of your group should take on the roles of Ceres, Iris and Juno, as well as director. You could adapt your script using one or more of the following techniques:

- Explore the story being told through movement, tableaux and sound only.
- Perform the story with a narrator reading out the modern script and a small cast acting out the words.
- Introduce a range of props, and incorporate them into the performance.
- Experiment with other sounds, including singing, clapping or musical instruments.
- Add more characters to reflect the growing scale of the masque.

Harmonious charmingly
magical, divinely harmonious

confines prisons
fancies fantasies

marred spoiled
wondered wonderful, capable of wonders
windring brooks winding streams
sedged crowns crowns made of reeds
ever-harmless always innocent
crisp rippling
temperate chaste, modest

sicklemen harvest workers
furrow harvest field

fresh pure
footing dancing

properly habited
appropriately dressed

minute appointed time
Avoid! leave instantly!
heavily sorrowfully

FERDINAND   This is a most majestic vision, and
Harmonious charmingly. May I be bold
To think these spirits?

PROSPERO   Spirits, which by mine art   120
I have from their confines called to enact
My present fancies.

FERDINAND   Let me live here ever;
So rare a wondered father, and a wife,
Makes this place paradise.

Juno and Ceres whisper, and send Iris on employment

PROSPERO   Sweet now, silence.
Juno and Ceres whisper seriously,   125
There's something else to do. Hush, and be mute,
Or else our spell is marred.

IRIS   You nymphs called naiads of the windring brooks,
With your sedged crowns, and ever-harmless looks,
Leave your crisp channels, and on this green land   130
Answer your summons, Juno does command.
Come, temperate nymphs, and help to celebrate
A contract of true love. Be not too late.

Enter certain nymphs

You sun-burned sicklemen of August weary,
Come hither from the furrow, and be merry,   135
Make holiday; your rye-straw hats put on,
And these fresh nymphs encounter every one
In country footing.

*Enter certain reapers, properly habited. They join with the nymphs, in a
graceful dance, towards the end whereof Prospero starts suddenly and
speaks*

PROSPERO   [*Aside*] I had forgot that foul conspiracy
Of the beast Caliban and his confederates   140
Against my life. The minute of their plot
Is almost come. [*To the spirits*] Well done! Avoid! No more.
To a strange, hollow and confused noise [the spirits] heavily vanish

The lovers comment on Prospero's anger. Prospero tells Ferdinand not to be troubled, because everything in the masque is ephemeral, and will fade. Prospero questions Ariel about Caliban and his accomplices.

Characters

Prospero's anger: real or pretended? (in threes)

Prospero is a magician with great powers: he is able to control the elements and command the spirit world. Yet the thought of Caliban's plot seems to trouble him deeply. Why?

- Draw up a list of possible reasons for his concerns. While doing so, think about whether he might just be pretending to be angry.
- Write notes for an actor playing Prospero, explaining your interpretation and suggesting how he should appear in the transition from the end of the masque up to line 158.

Language in the play

Prospero's famous speech

Lines 148–58 ('Our revels … sleep') are full of words with strong theatrical associations: 'revels', 'actors', 'baseless fabric' (the temporary scenery for a pageant play), 'globe', 'pageant', 'rack' (clouds painted on scenery). Just as the actors have vanished into thin air, so too will everyone and everything else. The lines have become famous as a metaphor for the impermanence of human life.

a Talk together about the mood of Prospero's speech. Why does it appear to be so elegiac (an elegy is a sad or reflective poem or song)?

b Work out how an actor could present the lines on stage. Suggest the tone of voice, which words to emphasise, where the actor should pause, and so on.

c You will find lots of versions of this speech online (it was even used in the opening ceremony of the 2012 London Olympics and the closing of the Paralympics). Which version do you feel is the most effective and why? Write down your thoughts in your Director's Journal.

d Why do you think this speech has proven to be so popular? Create a presentation in which you explain the power and significance of these ten lines.

e This is a beautiful speech, filled with rich images. Pick out three of your favourite phrases and explain why they are so striking.

---

passion strong emotion

works agitates

distempered extreme, lacking reason

movèd sort troubled state

revels dances

foretold you told you earlier

baseless fabric flimsy structure

all which it inherit all who live there now and later

pageant a scene in a play

rack tiny cloud

on of

beating disturbed

with a thought as soon as I think of you

cleave to unite with

meet encounter

presented acted (Ariel played Ceres)

varlets villains

FERDINAND   This is strange. Your father's in some passion
           That works him strongly.

MIRANDA   Never till this day
           Saw I him touched with anger so distempered.   145

PROSPERO   You do look, my son, in a movèd sort,
           As if you were dismayed. Be cheerful, sir,
           Our revels now are ended; these our actors,
           As I foretold you, were all spirits, and
           Are melted into air, into thin air;   150
           And like the baseless fabric of this vision,
           The cloud-capped towers, the gorgeous palaces,
           The solemn temples, the great globe itself,
           Yea, all which it inherit, shall dissolve,
           And like this insubstantial pageant faded   155
           Leave not a rack behind. We are such stuff
           As dreams are made on; and our little life
           Is rounded with a sleep. Sir, I am vexed.
           Bear with my weakness, my old brain is troubled.
           Be not disturbed with my infirmity.   160
           If you be pleased, retire into my cell,
           And there repose. A turn or two I'll walk
           To still my beating mind.

FERDINAND *and* MIRANDA   We wish your peace

                           Exeunt [*Ferdinand and Miranda*]

PROSPERO   [*Summoning Ariel*] Come with a thought! – [*To Ferdinand*
           and Miranda] I thank thee. – Ariel, come!

                      Enter ARIEL

ARIEL   Thy thoughts I cleave to. What's thy pleasure?

PROSPERO   Spirit,   165
           We must prepare to meet with Caliban.

ARIEL   Ay, my commander. When I presented Ceres
           I thought t'have told thee of it, but I feared
           Lest I might anger thee.

PROSPERO   Say again, where didst thou leave these varlets?   170

Ariel describes how he led Caliban, Stephano and Trinculo into a stinking pool. Prospero plans to punish them further, and reflects that Caliban is unteachable. Ariel hangs up gaudy clothes as a trap.

1 Ariel's torments: funny or cruel? (in small groups)

Lines 171–84 (to 'O'er-stunk their feet') are full of action and, like other episodes in the play, can be interpreted as both cruel and funny. Work on the following activities to explore how Ariel tormented the would-be assassins.

a One person reads Ariel's lines slowly. The other three members of the group act out the actions of Caliban, Stephano and Trinculo. Depending on the size of your groups, another person could play Prospero – how would he respond to what Ariel is telling him?

b Take it in turns to speak aloud just two or three words from each line in Ariel's speech. Choose the words that you feel convey most powerfully what happened to the conspirators.

Themes

Nature versus nurture (whole class)

Prospero's lines 188–90 explore an important theme of the play: can nurture (education, civilisation) change nature? Prospero regrets that, in spite of all his training and art, he has been unable to improve Caliban's nature ('a born devil'). He has succeeded in educating Miranda, but has failed with Caliban. So Prospero decides that he must further punish Caliban and the others ('plague them all, / Even to roaring').

- Hold a class debate on this statement: 'Nature, not nurture, is the major influence on our lives'. One group should argue that the natures we are born with determine what happens to us. The opposing group should argue that education can have a transformative effect on our lives. You might begin the debate by stating whether you think that human nature is essentially good or bad – or neither.
- Before the debate, take a vote on who agrees or disagrees with the statement. Take another vote after the debate has ended. Ask those who changed their minds to explain which arguments persuaded them.

red-hot excited

valour false bravery

smote struck

bending aiming

tabor drum

unbacked colts unbroken (never-ridden) horses

Advanced their eyelids opened their eyes

lowing mooing

filthy mantled scum-covered

O'er-stunk their feet created a stink that was worse than their feet

trumpery flashy clothes (the 'glistering apparel' of line 193)

stale decoy, con-trick

cankers festers

Even to roaring to a point where they cry out

played the jack with us messed us around, played tricks

in great indignation annoyed

ARIEL I told you, sir, they were red-hot with drinking,
So full of valour that they smote the air
For breathing in their faces, beat the ground
For kissing of their feet; yet always bending
Towards their project. Then I beat my tabor,   175
At which like unbacked colts they pricked their ears,
Advanced their eyelids, lifted up their noses
As they smelt music. So I charmed their ears
That calf-like they my lowing followed, through
Toothed briars, sharp furzes, pricking gorse and thorns,   180
Which entered their frail shins. At last I left them
I'th'filthy mantled pool beyond your cell,
There dancing up to th'chins, that the foul lake
O'er-stunk their feet.

PROSPERO   This was well done, my bird!
Thy shape invisible retain thou still.   185
The trumpery in my house, go bring it hither
For stale to catch these thieves.

ARIEL   I go, I go.   *Exit*

PROSPERO A devil, a born devil, on whose nature
Nurture can never stick; on whom my pains
Humanely taken, all, all lost, quite lost;   190
And, as with age his body uglier grows,
So his mind cankers. I will plague them all,
Even to roaring.

Enter ARIEL, *laden with glistering apparel, etc.*

Come, hang them on this line.
[*Prospero and Ariel stand apart*]

Enter CALIBAN, STEPHANO *and* TRINCULO, *all wet*

CALIBAN Pray you tread softly, that the blind mole may not hear a foot
fall. We now are near his cell.   195

STEPHANO Monster, your fairy, which you say is a harmless fairy, has
done little better than played the jack with us.

TRINCULO Monster, I do smell all horse-piss, at which my nose is in
great indignation.

STEPHANO So is mine. Do you hear, monster? If I should take a   200
displeasure against you, look you –

1 'Look what a wardrobe here is' (in threes)

Trinculo and Stephano are equally impressed with clothes, and take great pleasure in dressing up in the elaborate costumes they find on the line. The two men are fooled by appearances and, interestingly, it is only Caliban who recognises the garments as 'trash'.

a Research a number of occupations (a judge, a politician, a banker, a manual worker, a doctor, a soldier) and then discuss how much clothes tell us about the people who wear them.

b Find images of celebrities and talk about what their clothing choices reveal about the image they want to project.

c Create a display for your classroom that picks out key figures from different professions and historical periods. Analyse each element of their appearance, including crests or logos. You could begin with a school uniform. Make the display as visually attractive as you can and annotate it with appropriate quotations from Act 4.

d Consider how the exchange about clothes in the script opposite links to the theme of appearance and reality that runs through the play.

hoodwink this mischance compensate for this accident

fetch off rescue
be o'er ears drown

good mischief murder

aye ever

peer lord

frippery second-hand clothes shop

Put off remove

dropsy (a disease characterised by an excess of fluids)
dote thus on be infatuated with
luggage junk
Let't alone leave it where it is

jerkin short jacket

118

TRINCULO   Thou wert but a lost monster.

CALIBAN   Good my lord, give me thy favour still.
                    Be patient, for the prize I'll bring thee to
                    Shall hoodwink this mischance. Therefore speak softly –   205
                    All's hushed as midnight yet.

TRINCULO   Ay, but to lose our bottles in the pool!

STEPHANO There is not only disgrace and dishonour in that, monster,
                    but an infinite loss.

TRINCULO   That's more to me than my wetting. Yet this is your   210
                    harmless fairy, monster.

STEPHANO I will fetch off my bottle, though I be o'er ears for my
                    labour.

CALIBAN   Prithee, my king, be quiet. Seest thou here,
                    This is the mouth o'th'cell. No noise, and enter.   215
                    Do that good mischief which may make this island
                    Thine own for ever, and I, thy Caliban,
                    For aye thy foot-licker.

STEPHANO Give me thy hand. I do begin to have bloody thoughts.

TRINCULO   O King Stephano, O peer, O worthy Stephano! Look what   220
                    a wardrobe here is for thee.

CALIBAN   Let it alone, thou fool, it is but trash.

TRINCULO   O ho, monster! We know what belongs to a frippery.
                    [*Puts on a garment*] O King Stephano!

STEPHANO Put off that gown, Trinculo! By this hand I'll have that   225
                    gown.

TRINCULO   Thy grace shall have it.

CALIBAN   The dropsy drown this fool! What do you mean
                    To dote thus on such luggage? Let't alone,
                    And do the murder first. If he awake,   230
                    From toe to crown he'll fill our skins with pinches,
                    Make us strange stuff.

STEPHANO Be you quiet, monster! Mistress line, is not this my jerkin?
                    [*He takes down the garment*] Now is the jerkin under the line. Now,
                    jerkin, you are like to lose your hair, and prove a bald jerkin.   235

Stagecraft

The hunting of the conspirators (whole class)

The hunting of Caliban, Trinculo and Stephano can be a very humorous scene in the play. Have a go at performing it for the greatest comic effect.

- First, pick three students to direct three different versions of lines 250–60.
- Select the actors to play the main characters in each version, as well as a number to play the hunting dogs. Groups should rehearse independently of one another, but everyone should know what each director's ideas are before they begin rehearsing, to ensure variety.
- Perform your scenes with the rest of the class as the audience. Which was the funniest, and why? Write up your notes on these performances in your Director's Journal.

Characters

Has power gone to Prospero's head?

What do Prospero's lines 252–5 reveal about him by this point in the play?

- Read the lines in as many different ways as you can (joyfully, cruelly, 'tongue-in-cheek'). Then write some notes for the actor playing the part, advising him how best to perform this scene. How do you want the audience to respond to Prospero's words? Is there a way of making them anything other than purely vengeful?

1 An alternative view

Trinculo, Stephano and Caliban are clearly foolish (and drunk), but what are they *really* guilty of doing? Is it possible to defend them? Ariel tells us that they are roaring in pain, and so they have already been punished for a crime they are yet to commit.

- Imagine that you are representing these three characters in a court of law. Write a short statement for the defence, in which you argue that they should be set free
- Extend this activity by considering a case for prosecuting Prospero.

by line and level according to rule (plumb-line and spirit-level)

and't like if it please

pass of pate wisecrack

lime (sticky substance)

lose our time miss the opportunity by waiting

barnacles wild geese (in legend, geese grew from barnacles)

foreheads ... low (low foreheads were seen as a sign of stupidity)

lay to hold out

hogshead large cask

diverse various

Mountain ... Silver ... Fury ... Tyrant (dogs' names)

charge command

agèd cramps old people's cramps

pinch-spotted bruised by pinches

pard leopard

cat-o'-mountain wild cat

TRINCULO   Do, do; we steal by line and level, and't like your grace.

STEPHANO   I thank thee for that jest; here's a garment for't. Wit shall
not go unrewarded while I am king of this country. 'Steal by line
and level' is an excellent pass of pate: there's another garment for't.

TRINCULO   Monster, come put some lime upon your fingers, and away   240
with the rest.

CALIBAN   I will have none on't. We shall lose our time,
And all be turned to barnacles, or to apes
With foreheads villainous low.

STEPHANO   Monster, lay to your fingers. Help to bear this away where   245
my hogshead of wine is, or I'll turn you out of my kingdom.
[*Loading Caliban with garments*] Go to, carry this.

TRINCULO   And this.

STEPHANO   Ay, and this.

A noise of hunters heard. Enter diverse spirits in shape of dogs and hounds,
hunting them about, Prospero and Ariel setting them on

PROSPERO   Hey, Mountain, hey!

ARIEL   Silver! There it goes, Silver.   250

PROSPERO   Fury, Fury! There, Tyrant, there! Hark, hark!
[*Exeunt Caliban, Stephano and Trinculo, pursued by spirits*]
[*To Ariel*] Go, charge my goblins that they grind their joints
With dry convulsions, shorten up their sinews
With agèd cramps, and more pinch-spotted make them,
Than pard, or cat-o'-mountain.

ARIEL   Hark, they roar.   255

PROSPERO   Let them be hunted soundly. At this hour
Lies at my mercy all mine enemies.
Shortly shall all my labours end, and thou
Shalt have the air at freedom. For a little
Follow, and do me service.   260

                                                Exeunt

Looking back at Act 4
Activities for groups or individuals

1 Speedy themes

Act 4 contains many of the key themes in the play, but how well do you understand them?

- Form groups of ten. Look back through the act and write down five key themes on pieces of card. Now feed back to the rest of the class and, together, rank them in order of importance.
- Place five chairs in an outward-facing circle with a 'theme card' on the floor in front of each chair. Place another circle of five chairs around the first circle, so that you have two chairs facing each other with a 'theme card' between them.
- Sit facing each other and, for two minutes, discuss the theme on the card between you. When your time is up, those sitting in the inner circle move to the right and discuss the new theme they find there.
- When you have come full circle, discuss with your original partner any new ideas you might have come up with relating to the first theme.

2 Fathers and daughters

Prospero is the last in a long line of fathers in Shakespeare's plays who seek to control their daughters' choice of husband. Among others are Capulet in *Romeo and Juliet,* Baptista in *The Taming of the Shrew,* the Duke of Milan in *The Two Gentlemen of Verona,* Egeus in *A Midsummer Night's Dream,* Leonato in *Much Ado About Nothing,* Polonius in *Hamlet,* Lear in *King Lear,* Brabantio in *Othello* and Cymbeline in *Cymbeline.*

Shakespeare had two daughters, and it seems likely that he strongly disapproved of Thomas Quiney, the man who married his youngest daughter, Judith (although this was after *The Tempest* was written).

- One person steps into role as Shakespeare. The others question him about why he returns to the father–daughter theme so frequently in his plays. Begin by asking: 'Do you wish your relationship with Judith was like the one between Prospero and Miranda? Why?'

3 Prospero: thesis, antithesis, synthesis

Write an essay in response to this statement: 'Act 4 shows that Prospero is a megalomaniac tyrant, not a kindly old magician.' State one side of the argument (thesis), then put forward an opposing interpretation (antithesis), before bringing both positions together in a balanced and clear conclusion (synthesis). Remember to use quotations to support each of your points.

4 What are the other characters up to?

Several of the main characters in the play – Alonso, Sebastian, Antonio and Gonzalo – do not feature in Act 4 at all. What do you think they have been doing?

- Write a short script in which you imagine what these characters have been doing since the end of Act 3. Write your script in either modern prose or in Shakespearean verse using iambic pentameter.

5 Storyboarding the main action

Act 4 is short but pivotal. Make a storyboard of six to eight images that capture the main points of action in the correct order. Use lines from Act 4 as captions. Which scenes will you choose? What will you decide to leave out, and why?

6 To cut or not to cut?

Some directors cut lines and scenes from Shakespeare's play, but many consider this to be an act of cultural vandalism.

- Look at Act 4 and think about which lines you could delete without affecting the audience's enjoyment of the scene (could the whole of the masque be cut, for example?)
- Hold a class debate in which you discuss your choices and decide whether it is right to cut out lines from a play.

7 What will happen next?

It is widely believed that Shakespeare knew that *The Tempest* would be his final play. It would end a career in theatre unlike anything seen before or since. You are now about to read the final act of his final play.

- What do you think will happen? Jot down the main characters' names and then write two or three lines predicting their fates.
- As you write, think about which themes Shakespeare might have wanted to develop from the first four acts. What feeling might the playwright have wanted to leave us with as the curtain comes down for the last time?

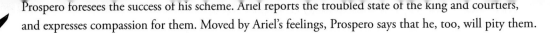

Write about it

Prospero: magician or scientist? (in pairs)

In the first few lines of this scene, Prospero uses the language of a magician and refers to charms, spirits and control of the natural world. His imagery is taken from alchemy, an early 'science' that attempted to change base metal into gold. Here, Prospero seems to see himself as an alchemist who carries out a 'project' (experiment), which will 'gather to a head' (come to the boil) if it does not 'crack' (fail). This language of alchemy, along with Ariel's description of its effect on the 'three men of sin', relates to the idea of a 'sea-change', where a person is transformed or purified through trials and suffering.

a Compile a list of Prospero's magic powers (his 'potent art') and contrast it with a list of the limitations of his power ('this rough magic').

b Write a paragraph or two in which you explore the kind of transformation that is prompted by Prospero's art. To what extent you see him as a benign magician?

1 Prospero's 'project' (in small groups)

Prospero's project seems to have a number of aims:

• Political ends – (i) uniting Naples and Milan through the marriage of Ferdinand and Miranda; (ii) the regaining of his own dukedom.
• Revenge – the punishment of Alonso, Sebastian and Antonio.
• Repentance – bringing the 'three men of sin' to repent their wrong-doings.
• Reform – overcoming, with nurture, the wicked nature of others.
• Self-knowledge – deepening his own humanity by overcoming his nature and putting mercy before vengeance.
• Reward – releasing Ariel from his service.
• Escape – leaving the island to return to Milan.
• Harmony – achieving unity and peace in personal, social and natural life.

Present Prospero's aims as a diagram, showing the relationships between them. Make it clear which aims you think are the most important. Add quotations and other aims if you can think of them.

---

project plan

gather to a head reach a climax

crack collapse, fail

Time … carriage time moves easily, free of burdens

you … charge you instructed me

line-grove clump of lime trees

weather-fends protects, acts as a wind-break for

till your release until you release them

abide … distracted all three are mad, out of their wits

eaves of reeds thatched roofs

works works on, agitates, stirs

affections feelings (both positive and negative emotions)

One of their kind also human

kindlier moved moved to act in a more human way, stirred to a greater generosity

Act 5 Scene 1
Near Prospero's cave

Enter PROSPERO *in his magic robes, and* ARIEL

PROSPERO   Now does my project gather to a head.
My charms crack not, my spirits obey, and Time
Goes upright with his carriage. How's the day?

ARIEL   On the sixth hour; at which time, my lord,
You said our work should cease.

PROSPERO   I did say so,   5
When first I raised the tempest. Say, my spirit,
How fares the king and's followers?

ARIEL   Confined together
In the same fashion as you gave in charge,
Just as you left them; all prisoners, sir,
In the line-grove which weather-fends your cell;   10
They cannot budge till your release. The king,
His brother, and yours, abide all three distracted,
And the remainder mourning over them,
Brim full of sorrow and dismay; but chiefly
Him that you termed, sir, the good old lord Gonzalo.   15
His tears runs down his beard like winter's drops
From eaves of reeds. Your charm so strongly works 'em
That if you now beheld them, your affections
Would become tender.

PROSPERO   Dost thou think so, spirit?
ARIEL   Mine would, sir, were I human.
PROSPERO   And mine shall.   20
Hast thou, which art but air, a touch, a feeling
Of their afflictions, and shall not myself,
One of their kind, that relish all as sharply
Passion as they, be kindlier moved than thou art?

Prospero decides on mercy rather than vengeance. He appeals to the spirits who have helped him to perform miracles, and declares that he will give up his magic powers.

1 Forgiveness, not revenge (in pairs)

Prospero's lines 20–30 have been seen by some critics as the moral centre of the play. Although his enemies have wronged him deeply, he will forgive them: 'The rarer action is / In virtue, than in vengeance.'

Is Prospero's assertion of his intention to forgive his enemies a result of Ariel's speech, or has this been his intention all along? How would you indicate your decision in a performance of this turning-point in the play? Work out a delivery of lines 1–32 as you consider the following options:

- Prospero is pleased to hear Ariel's description of the sorrow and repentance of his enemies, and reveals his plan for ultimate forgiveness.
- Prospero is moved by Ariel's declaration and feels compassion for the suffering wrong-doers, Alonso, Sebastian and Antonio. He visibly struggles with his conscience, then decides that he, too, feels merciful towards his enemies (line 20).
- Prospero is still angry and bitter, and reluctantly declares that he will forgive his enemies.

Characters

Prospero renounces his art (in small groups)

Prospero's lines 33–57 are a kind of invocation or spell, building dramatic effect as he calls on his spirits and describes the astonishing things they have enabled him to perform. His list culminates in a seeming paradox as he renounces his 'so potent art' and declares he will give up his 'rough magic' and become merely human again (line 51).

a Explore different ways of delivering the lines. Bring out the spell-like qualities, and the importance of Prospero's decision to give up his magic. At what point does he decide to 'abjure' his art? Is this spur of the moment, or did he know this earlier in this scene, or even earlier in the play?

b Step into role as Prospero and take turns to sit in the hot-seat. Answer questions from the rest of your group about why you have changed your view about your powers, and why you have decided to 'break my staff' and 'drown my book'.

---

high wrongs serious crimes

quick most tender part

nobler ... fury (Prospero sides with reason and opposes his fury)

rarer uncommon

sole drift single aim

standing still, not flowing, stagnant

with printless foot leaving no footprint

ebbing Neptune retreating tide

demi-puppets tiny spirits, half-sized puppets

green sour ringlets 'fairy rings' in grass

midnight mushrooms mushrooms that spring up in the night

solemn curfew evening bell rung at nine o'clock to signal night has come (after this time it was believed that graves opened and spirits roamed free)

masters ministers

azured vault blue sky

fire lightning

rifted split

bolt thunderbolt

promontory headland

spurs roots

rough violent, harsh

airy charm music which works a magic spell

plummet instrument for measuring the depth of water

Though with their high wrongs I am struck to th'quick,   25
Yet, with my nobler reason, 'gainst my fury
Do I take part. The rarer action is
In virtue, than in vengeance. They being penitent,
The sole drift of my purpose doth extend
Not a frown further. Go, release them, Ariel.   30
My charms I'll break, their senses I'll restore,
And they shall be themselves.

ARIEL   I'll fetch them, sir.   *Exit*

PROSPERO   Ye elves of hills, brooks, standing lakes, and groves.
And ye that on the sands with printless foot
Do chase the ebbing Neptune, and do fly him   35
When he comes back; you demi-puppets, that
By moon-shine do the green sour ringlets make,
Whereof the ewe not bites; and you, whose pastime
Is to make midnight mushrooms, that rejoice
To hear the solemn curfew; by whose aid –   40
Weak masters though ye be – I have bedimmed
The noontide sun, called forth the mutinous winds,
And 'twixt the green sea and the azured vault
Set roaring war. To the dread rattling thunder
Have I given fire, and rifted Jove's stout oak   45
With his own bolt; the strong-based promontory
Have I made shake, and by the spurs plucked up
The pine and cedar; graves at my command
Have waked their sleepers, oped, and let 'em forth
By my so potent art. But this rough magic   50
I here abjure. And when I have required
Some heavenly music – which even now I do –
To work mine end upon their senses that
This airy charm is for, I'll break my staff,
Bury it certain fathoms in the earth,   55
And deeper than did ever plummet sound
I'll drown my book.

1 Work out the staging (in small groups)

Copy and complete the table below to record your notes for performing the long stage direction and speech in the script opposite. Remember, none of the court party verbally responds to Prospero. He sometimes speaks to different groups or individuals, sometimes to himself and sometimes to the audience. As you complete the table, identify to whom Prospero speaks, his tone of voice, where he pauses and the gestures he could make.

Line	What might happen on stage
Solemn music … frantic gesture … stand charmed … (stage direction)	Alonso clutches his head and tries to run away, while Gonzalo tries to calm him down.
'spell-stopped' (line 61)	
'Fall fellowly drops' (line 64)	
'rising senses' (line 66)	
'Th'art pinched' (line 74)	
'You, brother mine' (line 75)	(e.g. in one production, Prospero slapped Antonio's face before addressing him in these lines.)
'inward pinches' (line 77)	
'I do forgive thee' (line 78)	(e.g. in one production, Prospero paused a long time before saying this line.)
'Begins to swell' (line 80)	
'yet looks on me' (line 83)	
'Fetch me' (line 84)	

A **solemn air** harmonious music (believed to cure madness)

unsettled fancy disturbed imagination, sick mind

Holy of high and reverend excellence

sociable to showing a human sympathy for

show appearance (Gonzalo's eyes show that he is weeping)

Fall fellowly drops weep friendly or sympathetic tears

rising senses (sunrise becomes an image of the lords' returning ability to perceive through their senses)

mantle cover, cloud

graces (both Gonzalo's virtues and the services he performed for Prospero at the time of his banishment)

Home fully

furtherer accomplice, assistant

pinched tormented

entertained harboured, gave way to

nature natural feelings

inward pinches torments of conscience

reasonable shore edges of reason

discase me remove my magic cloak

sometime Milan formerly duke of Milan

Solemn music. [Prospero traces out a circle on the stage.] Here enters
ARIEL *before; then* ALONSO *with a frantic gesture, attended by*
GONZALO; SEBASTIAN *and* ANTONIO *in like manner attended by*
ADRIAN *and* FRANCISCO. *They all enter the circle which Prospero had*
made, and there stand charmed; which Prospero observing, speaks

A solemn air, and the best comforter
To an unsettled fancy, cure thy brains,
Now useless, boiled within thy skull. There stand, 60
For you are spell-stopped.
Holy Gonzalo, honourable man,
Mine eyes, ev'n sociable to the show of thine,
Fall fellowly drops. The charm dissolves apace,
And as the morning steals upon the night, 65
Melting the darkness, so their rising senses
Begin to chase the ignorant fumes that mantle
Their clearer reason. O good Gonzalo –
My true preserver, and a loyal sir
To him thou follow'st – I will pay thy graces 70
Home both in word and deed. Most cruelly
Didst thou, Alonso, use me, and my daughter.
Thy brother was a furtherer in the act –
Th'art pinched for't now, Sebastian. Flesh and blood,
You, brother mine, that entertained ambition, 75
Expelled remorse and nature, who, with Sebastian –
Whose inward pinches therefore are most strong –
Would here have killed your king; I do forgive thee,
Unnatural though thou art. Their understanding
Begins to swell, and the approaching tide 80
Will shortly fill the reasonable shore
That now lies foul and muddy. Not one of them
That yet looks on me, or would know me. Ariel,
Fetch me the hat and rapier in my cell.

[Exit Ariel]

I will discase me, and myself present 85
As I was sometime Milan. Quickly, spirit,
Thou shalt ere long be free.

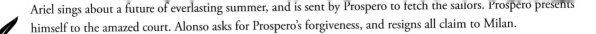

Ariel sings about a future of everlasting summer, and is sent by Prospero to fetch the sailors. Prospero presents himself to the amazed court. Alonso asks for Prospero's forgiveness, and resigns all claim to Milan.

Language in the play

Ariel's freedom song (in pairs)

Ariel looks forward to a life without winter or servitude, in which he will enjoy an endless carefree summer.

- Turn back to Caliban's song of freedom in Act 2 Scene 2, lines 156–62, and compare it with Ariel's. What do you notice about the sound echoes, rhyme, repetition and rhythm in both songs?
- What is the difference between the two songs in terms of the context, content, language and tone?

1 Images of speed

Ariel uses two remarkable images to convey the speed at which he will travel to release the sailors from their enchanted sleep: 'I drink the air before me' and 'Or ere your pulse twice beat'. A modern familiar image is 'as quick as a flash'.

- Make up two more images in the same style as Ariel's to convey the impression of amazing speed.

Stagecraft

How do the wrong-doers react?

Prospero first becomes visible to the court party at line 106. At that moment, the three men who had grievously wronged Prospero twelve years earlier see him in all his finery as the duke of Milan.

a Write detailed stage directions for how you think Alonso, Sebastian and Antonio should react. Invent a different reaction for each man when Prospero first appears (in lines 106–7) and then for when he embraces Alonso to show that he is real (in lines 109–10).

b Work through each phrase of Alonso's lines 111–20, and suggest a movement or gesture for each one.

---

attire him dress Prospero

couch rest, sleep

owls do cry (i.e. at night)

dainty (refers to Ariel's delicate beauty or grace, or the delicacy of the song he has sung)

enforce compel

drink the air before me fly incredibly swiftly

Or ere before

assurance certainty

enchanted trifle magical trick or hallucination

abuse harm or deceive

Th'affliction … amends my madness is ended

crave call for, demand

Thy dukedom I resign (Alonso immediately performs the act of satisfaction that is a sign of true sorrow and repentance)

my wrongs the wrongs I have done to you

ARIEL [*returns with hat and rapier,*] *sings, and helps to attire him*

ARIEL   Where the bee sucks, there suck I;
          In a cowslip's bell I lie;
          There I couch when owls do cry;   90
          On the bat's back I do fly
          After summer merrily.
          Merrily, merrily, shall I live now,
          Under the blossom that hangs on the bough.

PROSPERO Why that's my dainty Ariel. I shall miss thee,   95
          But yet thou shalt have freedom. [*Arranging his attire*] So, so so.
          To the king's ship, invisible as thou art;
          There shalt thou find the mariners asleep
          Under the hatches. The master and the boatswain
          Being awake, enforce them to this place;   100
          And presently, I prithee.

ARIEL   I drink the air before me, and return
          Or ere your pulse twice beat.   *Exit*

GONZALO   All torment, trouble, wonder and amazement
          Inhabits here. Some heavenly power guide us   105
          Out of this fearful country!

PROSPERO   Behold, sir king,
          The wrongèd Duke of Milan, Prospero.
          For more assurance that a living prince
          Does now speak to thee, I embrace thy body,
          And to thee, and thy company, I bid   110
          A hearty welcome.
                      [*He embraces Alonso*]

ALONSO   Whether thou beest he or no,
          Or some enchanted trifle to abuse me,
          As late I have been, I not know. Thy pulse
          Beats as of flesh and blood; and since I saw thee,
          Th'affliction of my mind amends, with which   115
          I fear a madness held me. This must crave,
          And if this be at all, a most strange story.
          Thy dukedom I resign, and do entreat
          Thou pardon me my wrongs. But how should Prospero
          Be living, and be here?

Prospero embraces Gonzalo. He reminds Antonio and Sebastian that he knows of their treachery to the king, but forgives them. Alonso regrets the loss of his son. Prospero says he has recently lost his daughter.

1 Still under the influence

The courtiers have had such extraordinary experiences that they are unwilling to trust their eyes. Prospero says that this is because they still 'taste / Some subtleties o'th'isle' (line 124). He is referring to sugar-covered sweets and pastries that were served after different courses during a banquet. These 'subtleties' were shaped like mythical figures or buildings, and made a kind of edible masque such as that in Act 4 Scene 1.

- If you had to design these 'subtleties' to represent the characters, events and themes of the play, what would they look like? Perhaps you might include a pastry in the shape of a harpy to represent judgement on the 'three men of sin', or a heart-shaped strawberry tart to represent the love between Ferdinand and Miranda.
- Consider the effect they would have on the person eating them: would they induce nausea, romance, hallucinations, or something else?

2 Forgiveness for the worst offender? (in pairs)

- Script a conversation between an actor and director who have different ideas about how to portray Prospero here. The actor thinks that Prospero says lines 130–2 between clenched teeth, as if he is forcing himself to forgive Antonio. However, the director thinks that Prospero's forgiveness is sincere and graciously given.
- As you write, talk with your partner about how you can develop these two interpretations of Prospero. Find quotations from the script opposite (and elsewhere in the play) to support each one.

Themes

'Loss', 'lost', 'lose' (in pairs)

a Take parts as Alonso and Prospero and read lines 134–52, emphasising the words 'lost', 'loss' and 'lose'. How many times are they used? What action or gesture could you use for each repetition to reflect the feelings of the two men in (supposedly) having lost their children?

b How would you instruct Prospero to deliver his lines. Remember that he could also be punning on the word 'lost' – in what other sense might he have 'lost' his daughter?

thine age your aged body

confined limited

You do ... subtleties you are still affected by the strange illusions

brace pair

justify satisfactorily prove

devil speaks (Sebastian is amazed that Prospero apparently knows of their conspiracy)

rankest worst

require demand as a right

point (the memory is imaged as a stab of recollection)

woe sorry

soft merciful, compassionate

like similar

her sovereign aid help of Patience

as late and as recent

dear grievous

means much weaker less to support me

PROSPERO	[*To Gonzalo*]　　　First, noble friend,	120

Let me embrace thine age, whose honour cannot
Be measured or confined.

　　　　　　　　　　[*Embraces Gonzalo*]

GONZALO　　　　　　　　　　　　Whether this be,
Or be not, I'll not swear.

PROSPERO　　　　　　　　　　You do yet taste
Some subtleties o'th'isle, that will not let you
Believe things certain. Welcome, my friends all. 125
[*Aside to Sebastian and Antonio*] But you, my brace of lords,
　　　were I so minded
I here could pluck his highness' frown upon you
And justify you traitors. At this time
I will tell no tales.

SEBASTIAN　　　　　　　　The devil speaks in him!

PROSPERO　　　　　　　　　　　　　No.
For you, most wicked sir, whom to call brother 130
Would even infect my mouth, I do forgive
Thy rankest fault – all of them – and require
My dukedom of thee, which perforce I know
Thou must restore.

ALONSO　　　　　　　　　If thou beest Prospero,
Give us particulars of thy preservation, 135
How thou hast met us here, who three hours since
Were wracked upon this shore; where I have lost –
How sharp the point of this remembrance is –
My dear son Ferdinand.

PROSPERO　　　　　　　　　I am woe for't, sir.

ALONSO　　Irreparable is the loss, and Patience 140
Says it is past her cure.

PROSPERO　　　　　　　　　I rather think
You have not sought her help, of whose soft grace
For the like loss, I have her sovereign aid,
And rest myself content.

ALONSO　　　　　　　　　You the like loss?

PROSPERO　As great to me, as late; and supportable 145
To make the dear loss have I means much weaker
Than you may call to comfort you; for I
Have lost my daughter.

1 'A most high miracle'

Everyone is astonished at the sight of Ferdinand and Miranda. In 2002, the Royal Shakespeare Company heightened dramatic effect by having the lovers drawn on to the stage while sitting in a boat.

a Suggest other ways in which the 'discovery' of the lovers might be staged to surprise both the courtiers and the audience.

b Explain how you would stage the three responses (from Alonso, Sebastian and Ferdinand) in lines 175–9, describing the tone and gesture each might have at this point. For example, the actor playing Sebastian has an opportunity to explore this character's complex response, which could be sincere or cynical – he certainly has much to lose by the recovery of Alonso's heir.

Themes

A game of chess (in pairs)

- Chess was an aristocratic game, and in literary tradition it is often associated with love because of its focus on strategic encounters – using moves and counter-moves to gain the upper hand in a way that could mirror the games lovers play or the proverbial battle between the sexes. The game could also be a reference to Prospero as a chess grand master manipulating all the players, and an ironic comment on the two lovers who think they are in control of the game.

- Talk together about the significance and symbolism of this game for the play and its characters.

mudded … bed buried in the mud of the sea-bed

admire wonder, marvel

devour their reason are open-mouthed in disbelief

do offices of truth perform their function truthfully

natural breath merely air

jostled … senses driven from your reason

strangely wonderfully, surprisingly

chronicle … by day story that requires much detail of daily life, or one that will take many days to relate

relation tale, narrative

abroad elsewhere on the island

requite reward, repay

discovers reveals

play me false deceive me, are cheating me

wrangle dispute, argue

If … twice lose if this is just another deceitful illusion that this island produces, I will lose my son a second time

compass surround

▲ In Shakespeare's theatre, Prospero probably drew back a curtain at the rear of the stage to reveal the lovers playing chess. At which line was this photograph taken?

ALONSO   A daughter?

O heavens, that they were living both in Naples,

The king and queen there! That they were, I wish   150

Myself were mudded in that oozy bed

Where my son lies. When did you lose your daughter?

PROSPERO   In this last tempest. I perceive these lords

At this encounter do so much admire

That they devour their reason, and scarce think   155

Their eyes do offices of truth, their words

Are natural breath. But howsoe'er you have

Been jostled from your senses, know for certain

That I am Prospero, and that very duke

Which was thrust forth of Milan, who most strangely   160

Upon this shore, where you were wracked, was landed

To be the lord on't. No more yet of this,

For 'tis a chronicle of day by day,

Not a relation for a breakfast, nor

Befitting this first meeting. Welcome, sir;   165

This cell's my court. Here have I few attendants,

And subjects none abroad. Pray you look in.

My dukedom since you have given me again,

I will requite you with as good a thing,

At least bring forth a wonder, to content ye   170

As much as me my dukedom.

Here Prospero discovers FERDINAND *and* MIRANDA, *playing at chess*

MIRANDA   Sweet lord, you play me false.

FERDINAND No, my dearest love, I would not for the world.

MIRANDA   Yes, for a score of kingdoms you should wrangle,

And I would call it fair play.

ALONSO   If this prove   175

A vision of the island, one dear son

Shall I twice lose.

SEBASTIAN   A most high miracle.

FERDINAND Though the seas threaten, they are merciful;

I've cursed them without cause.

[He kneels before Alonso]

ALONSO   Now all the blessings

Of a glad father compass thee about.   180

Arise, and say how thou cam'st here.

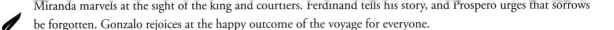
1 'O brave new world' (in pairs)

Miranda's words in line 182 reveal her essential innocence, but her wonder at the sight of so many strangers is charged with dramatic irony. The 'beauteous mankind' she sees includes usurpers and would-be murderers. Aldous Huxley's novel *Brave New World* uses Miranda's words ironically to describe an inhuman future world. Prospero's four-word response to his daughter's delighted exclamation is very ambiguous.

• Take parts as Miranda and Prospero and try different ways of speaking lines 181–4. Is Prospero's tone heavily ironic, gentle and sympathetic, dismissive or something else? Be prepared to explain what tone you think works best and give your reasons.

2 Design the pillars (in pairs)

Gonzalo enthusiastically recommends that the happy outcome should be recorded 'With gold on lasting pillars'.

• Take Gonzalo's words literally and design your own version of his 'lasting pillars'. Include on them your version of the inscription that Gonzalo has in mind (lines 206–13, from 'O rejoice').

Write about it

Sea-change

Gonzalo claims that each person has 'found' themselves as a result of the voyage and shipwreck (lines 206–13). Has each character really gained self-knowledge and understanding from their ordeal? Has each one changed?

a Turn to the list of characters on page 1. Write down each name. Alongside the names, note the way in which they have changed (or if they have not changed at all), and find quotations that support your ideas.

b Use this list to write a paragraph about the kinds of internal and external transformations that have occurred on the island.

---

goodly handsome, worthy
creatures people

Your eld'st ... hours you can't have known her for more than three hours

immortal providence divine fortune

renown glowing reports

second life (i.e. after his near-drowning)
second father (his father-in-law)
I am hers I am her father (in-law)

heaviness sorrow
inly inwardly, in the heart

chalked forth marked out as a course to be followed
amen so be it (Alonso agrees with Gonzalo's prayer)
Was Milan thrust was Prospero banished
issue descendants, children of Miranda
lasting pillars marble columns (such as Trajan's column in Rome, engraved with the stories of all his wars and victories)

When no man ... own when we had all lost our sense of our own identities

MIRANDA	O wonder!	
	How many goodly creatures are there here!	
	How beauteous mankind is! O brave new world	
	That has such people in't!	
PROSPERO	'Tis new to thee.	
ALONSO	[*To Ferdinand*] What is this maid with whom thou wast at play?	185
	Your eld'st acquaintance cannot be three hours.	
	Is she the goddess that hath severed us,	
	And brought us thus together?	
FERDINAND	Sir, she is mortal;	
	But by immortal providence, she's mine.	
	I chose her when I could not ask my father	190
	For his advice, nor thought I had one. She	
	Is daughter to this famous Duke of Milan,	
	Of whom so often I have heard renown,	
	But never saw before; of whom I have	
	Received a second life; and second father	195
	This lady makes him to me.	
ALONSO	I am hers.	
	But O, how oddly will it sound, that I	
	Must ask my child forgiveness!	
PROSPERO	There, sir, stop.	
	Let us not burden our remembrances with	
	A heaviness that's gone.	
GONZALO	I have inly wept,	200
	Or should have spoke ere this. Look down, you gods,	
	And on this couple drop a blessèd crown;	
	For it is you that have chalked forth the way	
	Which brought us hither.	
ALONSO	I say 'amen', Gonzalo.	
GONZALO	Was Milan thrust from Milan, that his issue	205
	Should become kings of Naples? O rejoice	
	Beyond a common joy, and set it down	
	With gold on lasting pillars: in one voyage	
	Did Claribel her husband find at Tunis,	
	And Ferdinand her brother found a wife	210
	Where he himself was lost; Prospero, his dukedom	
	In a poor isle, and all of us ourselves,	
	When no man was his own.	

1 Whom does Alonso have in mind? (in pairs)

Alonso condemns anyone who does not wish happiness for Ferdinand and Miranda: 'Let grief and sorrow still [always] embrace his heart'.

* Decide whether Alonso should look directly at Sebastian and Antonio as he speaks lines 214–15. Give reasons for your decision.

2 Reminders of the tempest (in pairs)

Gonzalo's friendly mocking of the Boatswain ('Now, blasphemy'), echoes what he said about the Boatswain in the first scene of the play (lines 25–9, 41–3, 52–3).

* Use these lines to explain why Gonzalo now jokes about 'on shore' and 'by land'. Also read what the Boatswain said in the first scene and decide whether or not he is really a blasphemer (someone who speaks irreverently about God or religion). Gonzalo's memory may be playing tricks on him.

3 The Boatswain's story (in small groups)

The story the Boatswain tells is full of striking detail (lines 230–40). He contrasts the horror of being rudely awakened by horrible noises with the sight of the master of the boat dancing for joy at the discovery of his undamaged ship.

a Prepare two tableaux to capture the events that the Boatswain describes. You might like to read specific lines aloud or provide sound effects for your tableaux.

b Discuss why Ariel or Prospero awoke the lower-class sailors in this way, compared to the heavenly music that rouses the aristocrats.

Characters

Ariel and Prospero

* Look at the snatches of private conversation between Ariel and Prospero in the script opposite, and think about their relationship at this point compared to earlier in the play.
* How would you want to stage their dialogue to show their feelings towards each other and the fact that no one else on stage can hear their conversation? Write stage directions at lines 225 and 240.

---

still always

amazedly in a bewildered fashion

swear'st grace o'erboard by swearing made God's grace abandon our ship

glasses hours measured by the hourglass (see also line 186)

gave our split reported wrecked

tight water-tight

yare ready to sail

tricksy capricious, resourceful

strengthen grow, increase

clapped under hatches imprisoned below deck

even now just now, a short while ago

several different, distinct

trim undamaged state

Cap'ring to eye her dancing for joy at the sight of his undamaged ship

On a trice immediately, in an instant

divided from them separated from the rest of the crew

moping in a daze

diligence hard worker, diligent one

more than ... conduct of something inexplicable

oracle ... rectify because these events are beyond nature, it will take a supernatural oracle to correct their understanding

ALONSO	[*To Ferdinand and Miranda*] Give me your hands:
	Let grief and sorrow still embrace his heart
	That doth not wish you joy.
GONZALO	Be it so, amen. 215

Enter ARIEL, *with the* MASTER *and* BOATSWAIN *amazedly following*

	O look, sir, look, sir, here is more of us!
	I prophesied, if a gallows were on land
	This fellow could not drown. [*To Boatswain*] Now, blasphemy,
	That swear'st grace o'erboard – not an oath on shore?
	Hast thou no mouth by land? What is the news? 220
BOATSWAIN	The best news is, that we have safely found
	Our king and company. The next, our ship,
	Which but three glasses since we gave out split,
	Is tight and yare and bravely rigged as when
	We first put out to sea.
ARIEL	[*To Prospero*] Sir, all this service 225
	Have I done since I went.
PROSPERO	[*To Ariel*] My tricksy spirit.
ALONSO	These are not natural events, they strengthen
	From strange, to stranger. Say, how came you hither?
BOATSWAIN	If I did think, sir, I were well awake,
	I'd strive to tell you. We were dead of sleep, 230
	And – how we know not – all clapped under hatches,
	Where, but even now, with strange and several noises
	Of roaring, shrieking, howling, jingling chains
	And more diversity of sounds, all horrible,
	We were awaked, straightway at liberty; 235
	Where we, in all our trim, freshly beheld
	Our royal, good and gallant ship; our master
	Cap'ring to eye her. On a trice, so please you,
	Even in a dream, were we divided from them,
	And were brought moping hither.
ARIEL	[*To Prospero*] Was't well done? 240
PROSPERO	[*To Ariel*] Bravely, my diligence. Thou shalt be free.
ALONSO	This is as strange a maze as e'er men trod,
	And there is in this business more than nature
	Was ever conduct of. Some oracle
	Must rectify our knowledge.

1 'this thing of darkness, I / Acknowledge mine'

(in pairs)

What does it mean for Prospero to 'acknowledge' Caliban? Many critics believe that, in lines 274–5, Prospero means more than 'Caliban is my servant'. They argue that Prospero accepts he also has an evil side to his nature, and believe his exile on the island has taught him that he must control his darker thoughts and desires.

a Experiment with reading aloud lines 271–5. In what tone does Prospero speak, and how might Caliban respond?

b Talk together about whether you think Prospero has an evil side to his nature. What kind of personal or spiritual journey might he have taken during the course of the play?

c Compose a soliloquy for Prospero, in which he reveals how his feelings and intentions towards his enemies – including Caliban, Antonio and Alonso – have changed because of his time on the island.

infest trouble, disturb

beating on worrying about

picked leisure a chosen moment

shortly single soon and in private

resolve you explain, make clear to you

Which … probable in a way that will make it seem likely to you

accidents things that have happened

odd extra or strange

Coragio courage

bully a term of endearment and familiarity

Setebos Caliban's and Sycorax's god

fine (in his ducal attire)

badges emblems (often worn by a nobleman's servants to identify them)

That could that she could

make flows and ebbs cause the tides

And deal in her … power use the moon's power without its permission

robbed me (i.e. by stealing the clothes that they now either wear or carry)

demi-devil half-devil

own acknowledge

▲ 'How fine my master is!' Caliban faces Prospero before the king and courtiers. Antonio and Sebastian are cynical to the end, commenting on Caliban's market value (just as Trinculo and Stephano did in Act 2 Scene 2).

PROSPERO   Sir, my liege,   245
Do not infest your mind with beating on
The strangeness of this business. At picked leisure,
Which shall be shortly single, I'll resolve you,
Which to you shall seem probable, of every
These happened accidents. Till when, be cheerful   250
And think of each thing well. [*To Ariel*] Come hither, spirit,
Set Caliban and his companions free:
Untie the spell.

                                                      [*Exit Ariel*]

[*To Alonso*] How fares my gracious sir?
There are yet missing of your company
Some few odd lads that you remember not.   255

Enter ARIEL, *driving in* CALIBAN, STEPHANO *and* TRINCULO
in their stolen apparel

STEPHANO   Every man shift for all the rest, and let no man take care
for himself; for all is but fortune. Coragio, bully-monster, coragio.

TRINCULO   If these be true spies which I wear in my head, here's a
goodly sight.

CALIBAN   O Setebos, these be brave spirits indeed!   260
How fine my master is! I am afraid
He will chastise me.

SEBASTIAN   Ha, ha! What things are these, my lord Antonio?
Will money buy 'em?

ANTONIO   Very like. One of them
Is a plain fish, and no doubt marketable.   265

PROSPERO   Mark but the badges of these men, my lords,
Then say if they be true. This misshapen knave,
His mother was a witch, and one so strong
That could control the moon, make flows and ebbs,
And deal in her command, without her power.   270
These three have robbed me, and this demi-devil –
For he's a bastard one – had plotted with them
To take my life. Two of these fellows you
Must know and own; this thing of darkness, I
Acknowledge mine.

CALIBAN   I shall be pinched to death.   275

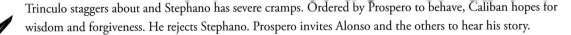

1 'I have been in such a pickle'

Trinculo and Stephano have little to say, other than expressing their aches and pains.

- Advise them on how to speak each line, how to behave and how to stage their exit. What do they do with their stolen clothes? How do they behave towards each other? (In one production, Stephano viciously rejected Trinculo's friendship.) In your Director's Journal, write detailed notes to the actors explaining what you want from them at this point in the play.

Characters

Caliban's last words – are they sincere? (in small groups)

Lines 292–5 are Caliban's final words in the play. Do they express his real feelings? Has he experienced some kind of moral transformation or a decisive change of heart? Does he lie to Prospero when he promises to behave well and 'seek for grace'? Does he threaten or strike Stephano? Has his attitude towards Miranda changed? What other questions do you have?

- Take turns as Caliban in the hot-seat and answer questions from others in your group. Remember to explain whether you have also gone on a journey of self-discovery, and why you said you were a 'thrice-double ass' to follow Stephano and Trinculo.

2 'Every third thought shall be my grave' (in pairs)

The play seems to be ending happily. Prospero looks forward to his departure for Naples, to the marriage of Ferdinand and Miranda, and to his return to Milan. But, like so much else in *The Tempest*, Prospero's line 309 is enigmatic. It could mean that he has a sense his life is drawing to a close, or that he will embrace his humanity and meditate on his mortality. Or it might have some quite different meaning.

- Talk together about how you interpret Prospero's thoughts and feelings at this moment, and suggest how you think the line should be spoken. Decide together what would work best on stage.

---

reeling ripe legless, staggeringly drunk

gilded 'em made them so red-faced, flushed

fly-blowing decay (because I'm pickled, i.e. preserved)

sirrah (term expressing contempt)
sore aching or sorry

disproportioned (Prospero refers to the idea that a person's outward appearance reflects the inner moral reality)

manners a person's habitual behaviour or conduct (especially in reference to moral character)

trim it handsomely prepare it richly for my guests

grace pardon, goodness

thrice-double (i.e. six)

this drunkard (Stephano)

this dull fool (Trinculo)

luggage stolen clothing

train followers

waste spend, pass

nuptial wedding ceremony

ALONSO	Is not this Stephano, my drunken butler?
SEBASTIAN	He is drunk now; where had he wine?
ALONSO	And Trinculo is reeling ripe. Where should they
	Find this grand liquor that hath gilded 'em?
	[*To Trinculo*] How cam'st thou in this pickle? 280
TRINCULO	I have been in such a pickle since I saw you last, that I fear
	me will never out of my bones. I shall not fear fly-blowing.
SEBASTIAN	Why how now, Stephano?
STEPHANO	O touch me not! I am not Stephano, but a cramp.
PROSPERO	You'd be king o'the isle, sirrah? 285
STEPHANO	I should have been a sore one then.
ALONSO	[*Gesturing to Caliban*] This is as strange a thing as e'er I
	looked on.
PROSPERO	He is as disproportioned in his manners
	As in his shape. Go, sirrah, to my cell;
	Take with you your companions. As you look 290
	To have my pardon, trim it handsomely.
CALIBAN	Ay that I will; and I'll be wise hereafter,
	And seek for grace. What a thrice-double ass
	Was I to take this drunkard for a god
	And worship this dull fool!
PROSPERO	Go to, away. 295
ALONSO	Hence, and bestow your luggage where you found it.
SEBASTIAN	Or stole it rather.
	[*Exeunt Caliban, Stephano and Trinculo*]
PROSPERO	Sir, I invite your highness and your train
	To my poor cell, where you shall take your rest
	For this one night, which, part of it, I'll waste 300
	With such discourse as I not doubt shall make it
	Go quick away: the story of my life,
	And the particular accidents gone by
	Since I came to this isle. And in the morn
	I'll bring you to your ship, and so to Naples, 305
	Where I have hope to see the nuptial
	Of these our dear-belovèd solemnised,
	And thence retire me to my Milan, where
	Every third thought shall be my grave.

Prospero promises a favourable voyage to Naples, and sets Ariel free. Alone on stage, Prospero admits that all his magical powers have gone. He asks the audience for applause, and for forgiveness to set him free.

Stagecraft

'Exeunt all': everyone leaves the stage

The way in which characters leave the stage may reflect how they think and feel at the end of the play. Write down your suggestions for each character. Use the following to help your thinking:

- **Ferdinand and Miranda** Do they look forward to the future with total pleasure? Do they leave before the others, or at the same time?
- **Antonio and Sebastian** They have not acknowledged their wickedness, and have spoken no words of repentance. How do they behave?
- **Alonso, Gonzalo and the courtiers** As king, does Alonso expect to leave first? How does his new-found repentance affect him?
- **Ariel** Ariel says nothing when Prospero gives him his freedom. Does he run delightedly into the darkness? Or does he react with anger and hatred, as in a 1993 production where he turned and spat in Prospero's face?

1 Prospero's epilogue – a plea for freedom

It was a convention in many Elizabethan and Jacobean plays for an actor to step out of role at the end and ask the audience for applause. This is the most complex epilogue in all of Shakespeare's plays because the figure on stage is both the character Prospero and the actor playing the part.

a Pick out all the puns and double meanings in the epilogue and discuss how you would show with gesture, tone of voice and position on the stage that it is both character and actor talking?

b Stage your own version of this epilogue. Try to capture the dramatic challenge Prospero throws out to the audience, as well as the ambivalent, complex ending the epilogue gives to the play itself.

Take affect, captivate

deliver all give an account of everything

auspicious gales favourable breezes

expeditious speedy

chick (a term that suggests the affection shown to a child)

charge task, responsibility

draw near approach (the cell)

charms magic powers

here (meaning both the island and the theatre)

deceiver (Antonio)

spell enchantment (by lack of applause)

bands bonds (imprisonment)

help ... hands by applauding (noise was thought to break a 'spell')

Gentle breath favourable comments or shouts of approval

enforce control

art magic power or theatrical art

prayer the success of my plea (or the audience's prayers)

indulgence pardon, applause

ALONSO   I long
To hear the story of your life; which must   310
Take the ear strangely.

PROSPERO   I'll deliver all,
And promise you calm seas, auspicious gales,
And sail so expeditious that shall catch
Your royal fleet far off. [*To Ariel*] My Ariel, chick,
That is thy charge. Then to the elements   315
Be free, and fare thou well. [*To the others*] Please you draw near.

Exeunt all [*except Prospero*]

EPILOGUE, *spoken by* PROSPERO

Now my charms are all o'erthrown,
And what strength I have's mine own –
Which is most faint. Now 'tis true
I must be here confined by you,
Or sent to Naples, let me not,   5
Since I have my dukedom got
And pardoned the deceiver, dwell
In this bare island, by your spell;
But release me from my bands
With the help of your good hands.   10
Gentle breath of yours my sails
Must fill, or else my project fails,
Which was to please. Now I want
Spirits to enforce, art to enchant,
And my ending is despair,   15
Unless I be relieved by prayer
Which pierces so, that it assaults
Mercy itself, and frees all faults.
As you from crimes would pardoned be,
Let your indulgence set me free.   *Exit*   20

Looking back at the play
Activities for groups or individuals

1 Harmony – or an uncertain future?

In traditional productions of *The Tempest*, the major themes of the play were presented as being harmoniously concluded. Prospero learns forgiveness and grants mercy to his enemies, reconciliation is achieved, all characters are set free from their enchantment and the future looks bright for everyone. In contrast, modern productions often end in a mood of uncertainty or even menace. In one production, Ariel returned to the stage after Prospero's exit, carrying his staff and clearly intending to take over the island and make slaves of Caliban and the spirits. In another production, Miranda's naïvety was highlighted and the 'brave new world' she thought she saw was questioned by Prospero's brisk remarks, to prevent any heart-warmingly happy ending to the play.

- Think about the final image you would want the audience to see in a modern production. Who is left as master of the island? Write a paragraph or two explaining how you think the play should end, giving reasons for your choice.

2 Press conference

On the return to Naples, a press conference is arranged. All the characters will be closely questioned by press, radio and television reporters. Take parts and stage the press conference. Prospero and Alonso may well have prepared a speech in advance to deliver at the quayside.

3 What happens next?

- **On the island** Step into role as Caliban or Ariel. Write the story of what has happened to you in the year since Prospero and the others sailed back to Naples.
- **Back in Naples** Step into role as Antonio, Prospero, Ferdinand or Miranda. Write about what has happened in the year since you arrived home.

4 Plot the action

A well-known theory of drama (based on the writings of the Greek philosopher Aristotle) states that if a play is to possess aesthetic harmony, it must observe the unities of action, time and place. This means that it should have a single action lasting less than twenty-four hours, taking place in a single location. *The Tempest* is unusual among Shakespeare's plays, as it observes the unities:

Time The action of the play takes place in under four hours (see Act 1 Scene 2, lines 239–41, and Act 5 Scene 1, lines 186 and 223).

Place Apart from Scene 1, everything takes place on the island.

Action All the sub-plots link neatly to the central plot of the usurpation of Prospero and his plan to regain his dukedom.

- Draw a timeline to represent 2 p.m. to 6 p.m., and place the various events in the play on it, from the shipwreck to the final scene. Remember, events in the sub-plot may occur at the same time as events in the main plot.

5 A mini-*Tempest*

- Write a summary of *The Tempest* in exactly 100 words. Now cut it down to exactly fifty words (try to stick to complete sentences); then cut it down to exactly ten words.
- Share these words with the class by posting them on a designated pinboard, by using sticky notes, or by posting them to a class website. Discuss the choices you have made.
- Now choose one word that you think captures the most important element in the play. Draw up a list of everyone's chosen words. Create a series of newspaper headlines (either for a tabloid or broadsheet paper) to capture the main events of the play using these words.

147

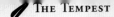

Perspectives and themes

What is the play about?

Imagine that you can travel back in time to around 1611. You meet William Shakespeare a few minutes after he has finished writing *The Tempest*, just before he takes it into rehearsal with his company, The King's Men. You ask him, 'What is the play about?' But like many great artists, Shakespeare does not seem interested in explaining his work, preferring to leave it up to others. He just says: 'Here it is. Read it, perform it, make of it what you will.'

There has been no shortage of responses to that invitation! *The Tempest* has been popular ever since it was first performed. The thousands of productions and millions of words written about it show that there is no single 'right way' of thinking about or performing the play. You will probably have noticed this as you looked at the photographs of different productions in this book. The play is like a kaleidoscope. Every time it is performed it reveals different shapes, patterns, meanings, interpretations. For example, you could think about *The Tempest* as:

- the dramatic story of a group of people who are shipwrecked in a great storm
- a moral tale representing the mental and emotional turmoil suffered by nearly all the characters as a spiritual journey that enables them to undergo a 'sea-change'
- a masque to entertain the court through spectacular theatrical effects, music, dance and mythology
- a play that comments on politics in seventeenth-century Europe, with a criticism of colonialism
- a romance play that contains elements of both tragedy and comedy, loss and recovery, mixing fairy-tale improbabilities and fantasies with love, magic, storms, feasts and miracles
- Shakespeare's last play, written as a farewell to the stage when he, like Prospero, gave up his art.

It is unlikely that Shakespeare had a single purpose in mind. As in all his plays, various interpretative standpoints allow different 'readings' of the play.

People have interpreted *The Tempest* according to a number of perspectives. These include:

Postcolonial perspectives – looking at power relationships between colonised cultures and people, based on the belief that no culture is better or worse than other cultures.

Cultural materialist perspectives – looking at the way politics, wealth and power strongly influence every human relationship.

Feminist perspectives – gender issues are politicised and critiqued from women's perspectives; this includes looking at the way women are represented and how gender can be both socially and symbolically constructed.

Psychoanalytical perspectives – looking at the unconscious and the irrational, as well as the impact of repressed sexuality and desire.

Liberal-humanist perspectives – freedom and human progress are the goals of life, and final reconciliation and harmony are possible.

◆ In pairs, talk about which of the perspectives described above would be most helpful in exploring *The Tempest* further. Then, in groups, choose a scene and experiment with staging it several times, focusing on a particular perspective each time. Take turns watching other groups' scenes and guess which perspective is being represented.

◆ Alternatively, by yourself or in pairs, write the script for a dialogue between two people with different perspectives on the play. Try to show how their conversation develops, and encourage them to agree or disagree with each other about the meaning of *The Tempest*.

Themes

Another way of answering the question 'What is *The Tempest* about?' is to identify the themes of the play. Themes are ideas or concepts of fundamental importance that recur throughout the play, linking together plot, characters and language. Themes echo, reinforce and comment upon each other – and the whole play – in interesting ways. For example, it would be difficult to write about illusion and magic without mentioning the themes of change and transformation or forgiveness and reconciliation.

As you can see, themes are not individual categories but a 'tangle' of ideas and concerns that are interrelated in complex ways. When you write about this play, you should aim to explore the way these themes cross over and illuminate each other, rather than simply listing each one. The key themes of *The Tempest* are outlined below.

Usurpation and treachery

The play portrays rebellions, political treachery, mutinies and conspiracies. All kinds of challenges to authority are made at all levels of society – on the boat, on the island and (in the past) back in Naples.

Nature versus nurture

Two major views of nature are explored in *The Tempest*. The first is that when left alone, nature grows to perfection and is inherently good. The second is that nature is inherently bad and therefore must be controlled and educated in order to become good.

The simple contrast between nature and nurture is questioned by Prospero when he says that Caliban is someone 'on whose nature / Nurture can never stick'. In this case, he suggests that it is not a question of whether nature is inherently good or bad, but whether or not nurture can have an influence on it.

Imprisonment and powerlessness

All the characters in the play suffer some kind of confinement, whether as a result of exile, unjust punishment, tests of character, the effects of magic, or their own conscience. Everyone yearns for freedom.

Forgiveness and reconciliation

For much of the play, it is not clear exactly what Prospero intends to do to his enemies. However, at the end he relents, deciding that forgiveness and mercy are better guides to human conduct than dominance and revenge.

Illusion and magic

The Tempest is full of magic and its effects: the opening tempest is itself an enchantment; music is everywhere; strange shapes, fantastic creatures and wonderful illusions appear; everything undergoes an alteration.

Colonialism and exploration

Tales that explorers brought back to England from what became known as the 'New World' are strongly echoed in this play. The Europeans set about what they believed to be their divinely ordained task of taking ownership of this New World. Gonzalo's vision of his 'commonwealth' – a dream of what the perfect, utopian society might be like – is in stark contrast to the realities of colonialism.

Sleep and dreams

Prospero sends Miranda to sleep, Ariel causes Alonso and Gonzalo to sleep, and Caliban's dreams are so wonderful that he longs to sleep again. The island itself also has dream-like qualities.

Change and transformation

The turbulence of the storm with which the play begins changes into the apparent peace and harmony of the ending. Many of the characters experience a 'sea-change': Alonso's despair turns to joy; Prospero's wish for vengeance metamorphoses into forgiveness; and Caliban's evil intentions become a desire for grace.

◆ Working in small groups, devise a tableau that shows one of the themes of the play. Present your tableau, frozen for one minute, for other groups to guess which theme is being portrayed.

◆ Imagine you are asked to explain what *The Tempest* is about by an eight-year-old child, and also by your teacher/lecturer. Write a reply to each of them, using these pages to help you.

Shakespeare's context and sources

One way of thinking about *The Tempest* is to set it in the context of its time: the world that Shakespeare knew. His imagination was influenced by many features of that world. Layers of dramatic possibilities within the script are built on past performances (such as morality plays, the Italian *commedia dell'arte* and English courtly masques), other literary texts (such as essays by Montaigne on cannibals, or by Erasmus on shipwrecks)

▼ The masque scene in the play may have been added later to celebrate a royal wedding.

and contemporary events or topical concerns (such as the voyages of exploration and settlement in Asia, Africa and America or the impending marriage of Princess Elizabeth). This layering gives Shakespeare's plays great depth, without limiting them to any single or specific social, religious or political meaning.

Writing for a king and his family

In 1611, the first recorded performance of *The Tempest* took place at the court of King James I of England and Ireland (and VI of Scotland). It is likely that the audience included James's wife, Queen Anne (a great patron of the arts), the heir to the throne, Prince Henry, the Princess Elizabeth and Prince Charles, their younger brother.

The play may be Shakespeare's response to the courtly masque, a form of theatre that developed – and was very popular – during King James's reign. Such entertainments contained spectacular theatrical effects, music, dance and bizarre and mythological characters. The king and his court would have expected a masque to end in the triumph of virtue, peace and beauty, with harmony restored under a rightful monarch. The wedding masque in Act 4 was possibly a later addition to the play to celebrate the princess's marriage to Frederick V in 1613. *The Tempest* was one of the many performances that were held in honour of the occasion.

There are other aspects of this play that would have interested the king and his family. Prince Henry was a great lover of adventure and exploration, although he was never allowed to embark on these voyages himself (it was considered too dangerous for the heir to the throne). He was always fascinated by the tales of discovery brought back by those who did go. He was also very religious, listening carefully to sermons given by those who commanded his attention. Christian ideas of repentance, forgiveness and the movement from sin to redemption through suffering are raised in this play.

These ideas were also found in earlier performances of the mystery and morality plays from the medieval dramatic traditions in England. Such plays portrayed the human struggle to choose between vice and virtue. They personified a range of vices (including the seven deadly sins) and virtues in stories of temptation and conflict between good and evil. The hero, often given a generic name like 'Everyman' or 'Mankind', must choose between them. Although the everyman is led astray by vice and wallows in sinfulness, he repents and is saved at the end of the play. The point of the plays is that although the hero succumbs to sin, God's mercy is always available to one who repents. In this way, the morality plays made the basic elements of Christianity accessible to those who were unable to read the Latin Bible for themselves. The plays taught people to beware the common vices that might tempt them, and to have faith in the mercy of God.

Magic and sorcery in *The Tempest*

In Shakespeare's England, the line between magic and science was not clearly drawn. A magus could be an alchemist (an early 'scientist' who attempted to change base metals into gold), or an astrologer, or a sorcerer (who supposedly communicated with the occult or spirit world).

When Shakespeare created Prospero, he may have had in mind Dr John Dee, a famous Elizabethan mathematician and geographer. Some of Dr Dee's work was genuinely scientific, but he was widely regarded as a magus. Shakespeare may also have had in mind the legend

of Dr Faustus, a magician who sold his soul to the devil in exchange for magical powers, and the play *The Tragical History of Doctor Faustus* – written by his contemporary Christopher Marlowe.

Prospero may be seen as a magus. He has devoted his life to secret studies in order to gain magical powers – what he refers to as his 'art'. When he decides to renounce these powers at the end of the play, he recalls all the miracles he can perform: dimming the sun, commanding the winds, making storms at sea, splitting oaks with lightning bolts and causing earthquakes. He can also raise the dead from their graves, raise and calm tempests, command his spirits to produce fantastic banquets and masques, make himself invisible, and control Caliban with cramps and pinches.

However, Prospero's magic powers are limited: he sometimes depends on luck to help him and although he can control the natural world, he cannot ensure that human nature will change. He cannot make Ferdinand and Miranda fall in love. He cannot cause his enemies to experience remorse and repentance for their deeds. His magic is unable to force Sebastian or Antonio to undergo a change of heart for their misdeeds. Despite its limitations – or perhaps because of them – Prospero's magic art is contrasted with the evil magic of Sycorax, Caliban's mother, and her god, Setebos. Whereas, arguably, Prospero uses his art to achieve virtue and goodness, Sycorax's sorcery is devilish and destructive.

◆ Just what were the books that Prospero brought with him from Milan, and from which he acquired his magic powers? Make up a list of possible titles for the books in Prospero's library. Choose one book and design it, showing the cover illustration, binding, contents page, and how the inside pages would be written and illustrated.

Sea voyages and shipwrecks

In writing *The Tempest*, Shakespeare was probably influenced by a true story that was the talk of London in 1610. In May 1609, a fleet of nine ships set out from England. Five hundred colonists were on board. Their destination was the newly founded colony of Virginia, where the settlers intended to begin a new life. They hoped for fabulous fortunes because of everything they had heard about the natural riches of America. But disaster struck.

The *Sea Venture*, the flagship carrying the expedition's leader, Sir Thomas Gates, became separated from the fleet in a great storm. The ship was driven onto the rocks of Bermuda – a place feared by sailors and known at the time as the Devil's Islands ('the still-vexed Bermudas' of Act 1 Scene 2, line 229). The rest of the fleet sailed on. On reaching Virginia, it sent back news of the loss of the expedition's leader with all of his 150 companions.

▼ **This Royal Shakespeare Company performance in 1998 used a model ship on stage during the opening tempest.**

For almost a year, England mourned. Then, in late summer of 1610, astonishing news arrived. The lost colonists had miraculously survived and reached Virginia. Apparently, the *Sea Venture* had run aground close to shore. All the passengers and crew had escaped safely, and were able to salvage most of the supplies from the ship. They had discovered that Bermuda was far from being the desolate and barren place of legend. It had fresh water and a plentiful supply of food in the form of fish, wild pigs, birds and turtles. The survivors had set about building two boats so that they could sail on to Virginia.

It seemed as if providence smiled, but human nature had soured the good fortune of the survivors, and mutiny had broken out. There were attempts to seize the stores. Malicious rumours had spread, and a bid was made to murder the governor and take over the island. Only after great difficulties had Sir Thomas Gates and his companions set sail for Virginia. Even then, two mutineers had elected to stay behind on Bermuda.

♦ Imagine you are William Shakespeare and that you met one of the survivors of the wrecked *Sea Venture* and heard their stories. What questions did you ask them and what were your own feelings about what they said? Write your diary entry to record what you learnt from this conversation and how it affected you.

Accounts of the tale

Shakespeare probably found the inspiration for *The Tempest* in pamphlets written in 1610–11, which described the misadventures of the would-be colonists. The following extracts suggest how Shakespeare's dramatic imagination might have been stirred by this miraculous tale of loss and rediscovery, of the benevolence of nature, and of mutinies against an island's leader.

> *On St James's day, a terrible tempest overtook them, and lasted in extremity forty-eight hours, and wherein some of them spent their masts, and others were much distressed.*
>
> From Council of Virginia pamphlet, 1610

An apparition of a little round light, like a faint star, trembling and streaming along with a sparkling blaze half the height upon the mainmast, and shooting sometime from shroud to shroud … And for three or four hours together, or rather more, half the night it kept with us, running sometimes along the main yard to the very end, and then returning …

The shore and bays round about, when we landed first, afforded great store of fish … Fowl there is in great store, small birds, sparrows fat and plump like a bunting, … White and grey heronshews [herons], bitterns, teal, snipes, crows, and hawks … cormorants, baldcoots, moorhens, owls and bats, in great store … A kind of web-footed fowl there is, of the bigness of an English green plover, or sea-mew…

Yet was there a worse practice, faction and conjuration afoot, deadly and bloody, in which the life of our governor, with many others, were threatened.

From a pamphlet written by William Strachey, 1610

♦ National newspapers did not exist in Shakespeare's time, so news was often spread by pamphlets. Can you see any elements of the characters and events of *The Tempest* in the descriptions above? Try to find quotations from the play that relate to the passages from the pamphlets. How has Shakespeare developed the ideas and language used here?

▼ An engraving showing the *Sea Venture* running aground in Bermuda in 1609.

Colonialism

The history of the colonisation of the Americas was a story of horror and savagery. For some, the prospect of unlimited wealth and a life of ease prompted them to embark on an adventure to the New World. In their greed, they viewed the native peoples as little more than beasts, fit only to be slaves. There are sombre echoes of this in the portrayal of Caliban. Others felt confident that they were educating the uneducated, bringing spiritual enlightenment to the heathen, and extending the domains of their European monarchs. Along with these aims went the profitable exploitation of what was seen as a wilderness, neglected by its existing inhabitants.

The native people must have viewed this invasion very differently. They saw their freedom vanish as they were forced into virtual slavery. Their lands were seized, their old religions destroyed and their languages eliminated. In *The Tempest*, Caliban is marked out as a savage because he cannot speak a recognised language such as English. He expresses the resentment of the enslaved:

> You taught me language, and my profit on't
> Is, I know how to curse.

This supplanting of his own language ('gabble' in Miranda's eyes) seems to articulate the deliberate process of linguistic control that English settlers often exercised not just in the new colonies, but also in neighbouring countries such as Ireland, Scotland and Wales.

Although some Europeans tried to uphold the principle of benign civilisation, the overwhelming evidence points to brutal conquest. European greed was a driving force of so-called 'civilisation' and the Europeans sought to profit by exploiting the rich resources of the New World. Such attitudes are reflected in the play when Trinculo (along with Stephano, Sebastian and Antonio) wonders how much money he could get for exhibiting Caliban at an English fair.

Europeans believed in their ethnic superiority over the native races of the Americas. These people were regarded as 'savages' or cannibals ('Caliban' is almost an anagram of 'cannibal'). But did the Europeans have the right to take possession, by gun and sword, of the native inhabitants' land? (Prospero's name is also almost an anagram of 'oppressor'). Resentful of Prospero's take-over, Caliban claims, 'This island's mine', to which Prospero replies, 'Thou most lying slave'.

The notion of social hierarchy was firmly fixed in the European mind, and most people believed it to be God-given. At the top of this social hierarchy was the king, who claimed to rule by divine right. Below him were aristocrats and courtiers, and so on, down to the lowest peasant. The 'masterless man' – a person without a superior – was seen as a terrible threat to social order. The European colonists of the New World brought back reports that the natives lived without a rigid social hierarchy. Caliban can be seen to represent this potential anarchy that needs to be controlled by harsh punishment.

In the eyes of Europeans, debauchery and vice flourished without control among the natives, and the marriage customs of Europe were unknown in the Americas. To the Europeans, such free love was abhorrent and Caliban's attempted rape of Miranda is evidence of his fundamentally evil nature, justifying constraint and harsh punishment. From the same viewpoint, Prospero's strict control of the sexual relations between Miranda and Ferdinand expresses a higher state of civilisation, characterised by restraint, abstinence and self-discipline.

There were other perspectives, however, and the French philosopher Michel de Montaigne wrote an essay entitled 'On Cannibals', arguing that 'savage' societies were in many ways superior to the 'sophisticated' civilisations of Europe. He introduced the idea of 'the noble savage' who was free from 'civilised' greed, ambition and lust for power: 'The very words that import lying, falsehood, treasons, envy, dissimulation; covetousness, detraction, and pardon were never heard.'

◆ Give Caliban a chance to tell his side of the story, starting with how the master/slave relationship quickly replaced that of teacher/pupil. Compose an account of what happened from his perspective.

▼ An engraving of Europeans arriving in the New World. Like Caliban, the native inhabitants often revealed the natural resources of their lands to the newcomers. Think about how the picture can help your understanding of *The Tempest*, and find one or two lines from the play to make a suitable caption.

Characters

How are characters created?

The process of creating characters is called 'characterisation'. In *The Tempest*, Shakespeare does this in three major ways:

By their actions – Prospero creates a storm; then he brings the courtiers to him and arranges for his daughter, Miranda, to marry Alonso's son Ferdinand.

By what is said about them – amongst other things, Prospero is called 'great master' by Ariel, 'dearest father' by Miranda, 'mine own king' by Caliban and 'the wrongèd Duke of Milan' by himself.

Through their own language – how they speak to each other and, through long speeches and **soliloquy**, what they say to themselves when alone.

Each of these is equally important. Long speeches and soliloquies allow us to gain a deep insight into the innermost thoughts of the speaker, but other characters provide us with different views, and a character's proof of their qualities. Every character has a distinctive voice, and part of Shakespeare's genius is to explore it while allowing it to both change (as events affect the character's mind) and remain unique and recognisable.

Characters evolve over the course of the play – some more than others. However, unlike many of Shakespeare's plays (particularly the tragedies), *The Tempest* does not demonstrate particularly extreme changes in character.

◆ In small groups, discuss which characters change over the course of the play. Which of their actions most influence how you view them?

◆ Which speeches by Prospero and Caliban offer the greatest insight into their personalities? Collect key quotations that show the changes in these two characters over the course of the play. Display your choice of quotations on a large piece of paper, with images that symbolise these significant moments.

Prospero

Historically, Prospero was portrayed as a well-intentioned magician – a serene old man whose 'project' was to restore harmony and achieve reconciliation. However, over the past fifty years, many productions have shown Prospero as a much more ambiguous figure. He has been depicted as harsh and demanding, impatient and deeply troubled. Opinions about this character vary widely. Below are some interpretations of Prospero.

Enabler – Prospero is Latin for 'I cause to succeed, make happy and fortunate'. Bearing this definition in mind, how appropriate do you think Prospero's name is?

Magus and scholar – Prospero successfully learns to practise magic. His books and his spirits enable him to control the natural world, but to what extent can he control human nature – his own and others'?

Prince – Prospero's self-centred pursuit of study caused him to neglect his civic duties as duke of Milan, and subsequently led to his overthrow. When he is reinstated in this position, will he devote himself single-mindedly to good government ('Every third thought shall be my grave')?

Father – is Prospero a loving, kind and devoted father to Miranda? Or is he bad-tempered, dictatorial and irritable?

Revenger – Prospero pardons his enemies at the end of the play, but was his original plan to seek revenge for his overthrow and banishment?

Man – at the end of the play, Prospero admits to his weakness as a fallible human being:

> Now my charms are all o'erthrown,
> And what strength I have's mine own

What has he learned in the course of the play?

Master – Prospero controls Caliban harshly with cramps and pinches. He does not have a single good word to say about his slave. Is Prospero a colonialist exploiter, or a benevolent ruler of the island?

Actor-manager – Prospero is like a theatre director. He stages the opening tempest. He ensures that Gonzalo and Alonso sleep, thus provoking a murder attempt. He is the unseen observer of his daughter and his enemies.

He also produces the banquet and the masque. Is Prospero the puppet-master? Are all the other characters merely his 'actors'?

Shakespeare – Some people believe that Shakespeare wrote the part of Prospero as a self-portrait, particularly in his farewell to his 'art' at Act 5 Scene 1, lines 33–57. Knowing what you know about Shakespeare, how does this affect your reading of this character?

◆ Rank these interpretations in order, with the one that best matches your own understanding of Prospero at the top.

◆ In small groups, discuss which of these interpretations of Prospero gives you the greatest insight into his character. Share your discussions with the rest of the class.

◆ Look at the production photograph of Prospero below. Compare how he is presented here with his portrayal in the pictures elsewhere in this book. Write a description of how you would present this character on stage.

Ariel

Ariel is described in the list of characters as 'an airy spirit', and has been played by both male and female actors. Ariel appears in different guises: a flaming light in the storm, a nymph of the sea, a harpy at the banquet, Ceres in the masque. At Prospero's command, Ariel performs near-impossible feats, such as fetching 'dew / From the still-vexed Bermudas', treading 'the ooze / Of the salt deep' and running 'upon the sharp wind of the north'.

Imprisoned by Sycorax for refusing to obey her orders, and freed by Prospero's magic, Ariel yearns for freedom throughout the play. Prospero's attitude to his spirit-servant is ambiguous. Sometimes he seems affectionate, calling Ariel 'bird', 'chick', 'my fine spirit'. But, at other times, he calls Ariel 'moody' or 'malignant thing'. When Ariel demands 'my liberty', Prospero threatens him with twelve more years of imprisonment.

Ariel's language often expresses rapid movement and breathless excitement. There is a childlike eagerness to please in 'What shall I do? Say what? What shall I do?' But there is greater depth to the character if we look closer: is it Ariel who teaches Prospero forgiveness and pity? Describing the plight of Prospero's enemies, Ariel says that the sight of them would make Prospero feel compassion (Act 5 Scene 1, lines 18–20):

ARIEL   *That if you now beheld them, your affections*
        Would become tender.

PROSPERO   *Dost thou think so, spirit?*

ARIEL   *Mine would, sir, were I human.*

PROSPERO   *And mine shall.*

Some critics think that Ariel exists only in Prospero's mind. Others see him as Prospero's chief informer and secret policeman. At the end of one production, Ariel picked up Prospero's broken staff, put it together again, and assumed the role of ruler of the island.

◆ **What is your view of Ariel? Think about the following:**

• Male, female – or something 'other'? Some productions emphasise Ariel's asexuality. Are there benefits to seeing Ariel as either male, female or androgynous?

• Does Ariel serve Prospero with eager and spontaneous willingness, or with reluctance and bad temper?

• Does Ariel love Prospero, or fear and detest him, or feel other emotions? Do these feelings change? If so, where exactly are these turning points?

• What are Prospero's feelings for Ariel: genuine love, or a harsh master's demand to have his every wish instantly performed?

◆ After considering the questions above, design a poster in which you visualise Ariel. You may find it helps to base your representation on one line or an episode from the play. Find quotations to support your interpretations and use them on your poster.

▲ 'On the bat's back I do fly.' A poster advertising a theatre production of *The Tempest*.

Caliban

Caliban is described as a 'savage and deformed slave' in the list of characters, and in all kinds of uncomplimentary ways in the play – 'filth', 'hag-seed', 'misshapen knave' and 'monster'. On stage, he has been played as a lizard, a dog, a monkey, a snake and a fish. In one production, he was a tortoise, and was turned over onto his back by Prospero when he became unruly.

In the eighteenth century, the comic aspects of the role were emphasised. Caliban was a figure of fun, not to be taken seriously. In recent times, performances have emphasised Caliban's human and tragic qualities, not just his wickedness. He has increasingly been seen as a native dispossessed of his language and land by a colonial exploiter.

To help you form your own view of Caliban, think about each of the following:

Victim? A ruthless exploiter takes over Caliban's island, forcing him into slavery. He is seen by the shipwrecked Europeans as an opportunity to make money.

Savage? Caliban is brutish and evil by nature, incapable of being educated or civilised ('on whose nature / Nurture can never stick'). His plot against Prospero reflects his violent and vindictive nature.

Servant? Caliban deserves to be a servant. He merely exchanges a harsh master (Prospero) for a drunken one (Stephano), and wants to serve as a 'foot-licker'.

Contrast? Caliban's function in the play is to act as a contrast to other characters. For example, lust versus true love (Ferdinand), or the natural malevolence he exhibits towards Prospero versus the civilised and calculating evil of Antonio.

Noble savage? Until Prospero arrived, Caliban lived in natural freedom. He loves the island, and his language eloquently expresses some of the most haunting poetry in the play when he responds to Ariel's music: 'the isle is full of noises'.

Symbol of wickedness? Shakespeare's contemporaries believed that deformity was a sign of the wickedness of parents. Prospero claims that Caliban is the son of a witch and the devil. It is also suggested that he tried to rape Miranda. How would you define 'wicked' in the context of the play?

Term of abuse? The word 'Caliban' has entered the English language as a derogatory description. To call someone 'a Caliban' is to imply that they are wicked, violent and sinister.

Sensitive and perceptive? In Act 3 Scene 2, it is Caliban who describes the island so beautifully, and it is he who in Act 4 sees the clothes that Trinculo and Stephano are so taken by as 'trash'. Having suffered so much by being judged on his appearance, Caliban is able to look deeper.

Other characters

Miranda

Miranda appears to be a pure and innocent character, obedient to her father, Prospero. Her first words express compassion for the shipwreck's victims. She falls in love at first sight with Ferdinand (just as Prospero had hoped). She seems like a maiden in a fairy-tale or romance.

However, Shakespeare complicates her character. She assures her father that she is listening to his story, but the rest of the play suggests that she has not paid attention (because she never links Ferdinand or the other shipwrecked characters with the story Prospero has told her). She directs an apparently uncharacteristic torrent of abuse at Caliban, and she stands up for Ferdinand when Prospero treats him harshly. She also disobeys her father by secretly meeting Ferdinand and telling him her name.

Feminist critics have seen Miranda – the only female character we see on stage – as a feeble representation of women, who seemingly exists to serve first her father and then Ferdinand.

This lack of any distinct female identity is extended to the other women referred to in the text: Caliban's mother, Sycorax, Miranda's mother, and Alonso's daughter Claribel are all marginalised and often subservient to male desires and demands.

Sycorax alone seems to have had some power, but when the play begins she is already dead and demonised by Prospero. Claribel has been given away by Alonso to the king of Tunis (a parallel, perhaps, with the interracial 'union' between Miranda and Caliban that Prospero has thwarted), and Miranda's mother is barely present as a memory for her daughter.

Although for some critics, then, Miranda is barely realised as a character, she does draw together many complex ideas. Many modern directors and actors seek to explore this on stage. It is Miranda who is seen as a possession by Prospero, and one who is given away by him so that he can regain power once removed from the island. It is she who is used by others like the pawn in the game of chess she plays with Ferdinand.

◆ Think about how complex this character is. How would you describe Miranda's qualities to someone who has not read the play?

Ferdinand

Ferdinand also seems to be a stock figure of romance: the noble prince who undergoes harsh ordeals, but finally marries a pure maiden. He is first seen enchanted by Ariel's music, but still grieving for the father whom he believes is drowned. He falls instantly in love with Miranda, and patiently endures the hard tasks that Prospero imposes on him. His betrothal to Miranda and his final words help strengthen the reconciliation of Alonso with Prospero.

Gonzalo

Gonzalo appears to be precisely as he is described in the list of characters – 'an honest old councillor'. Just as he had helped Prospero, he is loyal to Alonso, seeking to cheer him in his grief. His integrity and sincerity contrast with Sebastian's and Antonio's treachery and cynicism, and he resists their mocking. Always unselfish and optimistic, at the play's end he rejoices that harmony has been restored. He is often played as a rather elderly, ineffectual idealist, easily mocked by Antonio and Sebastian.

Antonio and Sebastian

Antonio seems to be a selfish schemer, a character who betrayed his brother Prospero and seized his dukedom. On the island, he and Sebastian mock Gonzalo, then plot together to kill Alonso. When that plot is foiled by Ariel, they again agree to carry out the assassination. Highly disturbed by Ariel's accusation, they resolve to fight, but become spellbound until Prospero releases them from their distraction. Neither man expresses remorse for his evil deeds and intentions. Their last words in the play are as cynical as their first. Is it possible to distinguish between the two characters? Is Antonio the more manipulative, or do we dislike Sebastian more because he is so easily led?

Stephano and Trinculo

These are the comic counterparts of Antonio and Sebastian. Although they add much humour to the play, they both hope to make money out of Caliban, and the drunken Stephano makes him his slave. At Caliban's prompting, Stephano agrees to murder Prospero and become king of the island. Their absurd desire to dress in gaudy clothing leads to their downfall, and – hunted by Prospero's spirits – they end up dishevelled and drunk, their foolishness clear to everyone.

What do you think these characters offer the audience beyond the obvious humour? Do you think that we judge them too quickly (and too harshly)?

▼ Stephano and Trinculo (pictured here with Ariel – with his arms raised – and Caliban) provide the comedic element of the play.

- Study the pictures on these pages. In groups, talk about what each of these images conveys about the characters.

- One person steps into role as one of the characters and takes his or her place in the hot-seat. Group members ask this character questions about why they behave the way they do. Keep the tightly focused so that each character has the same amount of time.

- In pairs, write or improvise a dialogue between Prospero and another character, reflecting on their relationship and what they want or need from each other. Other members of your class could watch and give feedback, commenting on how true to the spirit of both characters your interpretations are.

- In small groups, write one question each on the relationship between any two characters. Use questions such as 'To what extent would you agree that …?' Choose from Prospero, Caliban, Ariel or Miranda. Select the strongest overall question and

draw up a group answer in the form of an essay plan. Deliver your essay plans in a presentation to the rest of the class. Keep the presentation succinct, using six to eight slides, with each slide representing a different part of the essay. The slides should contain only key words: it is up to you to talk the class through your answer in more detail.

How real are the characters?

- The Shakespeare critic L. C. Knights wrote a famous essay entitled 'How many children had Lady Macbeth?' In it, he mocked the way that some people approach a study of Shakespeare's plays as if the characters were real human beings. How do you feel about what L. C. Knights claims? In groups, discuss your views. Do you see the characters not just as figures in a play, but as real human beings with past lives and familiar emotions?

The language of *The Tempest*

Imagery

The Tempest abounds in **imagery** (sometimes called 'figures' or 'figurative language'). Imagery is created by vivid words and phrases that conjure up emotionally charged mental pictures or associations. Imagery provides insight into character, and stirs the audience's imagination. It deepens the dramatic impact of particular moments or moods.

In Act 2 Scene 1, as Antonio tempts Sebastian with his murderous plan, he says that he will kill Alonso with 'this obedient steel', instead of 'this sword'. When he assures Sebastian that Naples is so far away from Tunis that it would take a message many years to travel the distance, he uses a striking image: 'till newborn chins / Be rough and razorable' (the time from when a baby boy is born until he begins to shave).

The imagery used to describe change is made more striking in the image that extends over several lines in Ariel's account of the 'sea-change' undergone by people when they die. Ariel also describes how the skeleton of the drowned king has turned to coral and his eye sockets have filled with pearls:

Full fathom five thy father lies,
Of his bones are coral made;
Those are pearls that were his eyes;
Nothing of him that doeth fade,
But doth suffer a sea-change
Into something rich and strange.

The sea, dreams and spirits are recurring images in the play and contribute to its strange, dream-like world that causes both terror and wonder.

◆ **In role as a film director, write out your ideas for how the imagery in certain passages might be visualised in a film production. Prepare a storyboard or part of a film script to illustrate your ideas.**

The images that recur throughout the play include:

The sea The play begins in a storm and ends with the promise of calm seas. In between, images of the sea frequently occur: 'sea-sorrow', 'sea-change', 'sea-swallowed', 'never-surfeited sea' (suggesting the infinite appetite of the ocean), 'still-closing waters', and so on. Prospero speaks of the tempest that he and Miranda endured when they were banished from Milan: 'th'sea, that roared to us'. In Act 2 Scene 1, lines 217–24, the sea's ebb and flow is reflected in the exchange in which

Antonio tempts Sebastian: 'I am standing water', 'I'll teach you how to flow', 'Ebbing men, indeed'. In Act 5 Scene 1, lines 79–81, Prospero – about to release his enemies from their enchantment back to sanity – declares:

> *Their understanding*
> *Begins to swell, and the approaching tide*
> *Will shortly fill the reasonable shore*

The theatre Shakespeare's interest in the theatre is evident throughout *The Tempest*. There are the spectacular dramatic events of the shipwreck, the banquet and the masque. The language is full of echoes of acting and plays. Ariel is like a stage-manager as he 'performs' the tempest and arranges the banquet and the masque. When he seizes control in Milan, Antonio is like an actor who would 'have no screen between this part he played, / And him he played it for' (Act 1 Scene 2, lines 107–8). Later, as he plots Alonso's murder, Antonio uses the language of the theatre: 'cast … perform … act … prologue … discharge' (Act 2 Scene 1, lines 247–50). Prospero reflects on the way in which life itself is like a stage pageant, whose actors and theatre, 'the great globe itself', vanish into thin air (Act 4 Scene 1, lines 147–58).

Nature The play's language evokes the rich variety of the natural world: sea, air, earth and wildlife, thunder and lightning, wind and roaring water. Every scene contains aspects of nature, both benign and threatening. Caliban's language expresses his intimate knowledge and love of the island as he describes the 'fresh springs, brine-pits, barren place and fertile', 'fresh-brook mussels, withered roots and husks', 'pig-nuts' and 'jay's nest', while Ariel delights that he has led the drunken conspirators through 'Toothed briars, sharp furzes, pricking gorse, and thorns' to the 'filthy mantled pool'.

Verse and prose

The verse of *The Tempest* is mainly **blank verse**: unrhymed verse with a five-beat rhythm called iambic pentameter. This is a rhythm or metre in which each line has five **feet** (groups of syllables) called **iambs**, which have one unstressed (×) and one stressed (/) syllable:

× / × / × / × / × /

So, king, go safely on to seek thy son.

By the time he came to write *The Tempest* (around 1610), Shakespeare used great variation in his verse. He sometimes wrote lines of more or fewer than ten syllables, sometimes changed the pattern of stresses in a line, and sometimes used rhyming couplets for effect. He ensured that the rhythm of the verse was appropriate to the meaning and mood of the speech: reflective, fearful, apprehensive, anguished or confused.

These rhythmic patterns are what distinguish verse from prose, not whether the lines rhyme. Prose is different from blank verse: it is everyday language with no specific rhythm, metric scheme or rhyme. Shakespeare uses prose to break up the verse in his plays, to signify characters' madness or low status, or to draw attention to changes in plot or character. It is easy to tell the difference: verse lines all begin with a capital letter and the lines do not reach the other side of the page, whereas prose passages have lines that stretch across the page and only use capital letters at the beginning of sentences.

Shakespeare also used **caesura** and **enjambement** to add to the rhythm of his blank verse. A caesura is where a phrase ends in the middle of a line to create a pause or a break in the dialogue or action. With enjambement, the phrase carries over into the next line of poetry. In so doing, phrases spill over and build up from one line to the next, increasing the emotional or dramatic impact of the script.

Prose was traditionally used by comic and low-status characters. High-status characters generally use verse. There are exceptions, however. Sebastian and Antonio, despite their high status, use prose as they taunt Gonzalo. Similarly, Caliban, despite his very low status, speaks verse – some of it of extraordinary beauty. He uses prose in his first encounter with Stephano and Trinculo (low-status and comic characters), but ends the scene with haunting poetry as he resolves to leave Prospero and serve Stephano:

> *Be not afeared; the isle is full of noises,*
> *Sounds, and sweet airs, that give delight and hurt not.*

◆ **The human heartbeat has an iambic rhythm. Put your hand on your heart to hear the basic rhythm of weak and strong stresses.**

◆ **Choose a verse speech. Iambic pentameter, with five stresses, will be easy to find, while tetrameter, with four beats, is found only in the songs. Explore ways** of speaking it to emphasise the metre. You could clap your hands, tap the desk or walk five paces to accompany each line, for example. Afterwards, write eight or more lines of your own in the same style.

Metaphor, simile and personification

Shakespeare's imagery uses **metaphor**, **simile** or **personification**. All are comparisons.

A simile compares one thing to another using 'like' or 'as'. For example, Trinculo exclaims that Caliban 'smells like a fish'. Ariel compares Gonzalo's weeping to rain falling from a thatched roof: 'His tears runs down his beard like winter's drops / From eaves of reeds'.

A metaphor is also a comparison, suggesting that two dissimilar things are the same. Prospero describes the leaky boat in which he and Miranda were set adrift as 'A rotten carcass of a butt'. His image for the tears he wept on the voyage becomes 'I have decked the sea with drops full salt'.

Personification turns all kinds of things into persons, giving them human feelings or attributes, such as when Prospero declares 'bountiful Fortune, / Now my dear lady, hath mine enemies / Brought to this shore'. Here, he sees Fortune as his goddess or his friend.

Antithesis and repetition

Antithesis is the opposition of words or phrases to each other, and it expresses the conflict that is at the heart of the play and that is the essence of all drama. Ferdinand, discovering his father is alive, not drowned, gratefully exclaims, 'Though the seas threaten, they are merciful'. A similar antithesis is set up between Caliban and Ariel, who represent earth versus air, and Prospero and Sycorax, where the former's magic 'art' is superior to the witch's evil sorcery. Antithesis is especially powerful in *The Tempest*, where good is set against evil and where illusion and magic are major themes.

Shakespeare used **repetition** to give his language great dramatic force. Perhaps the most obvious example of repetition is found in Ariel's songs, which please the ear by being rich in the repeated sounds of rhyme and the hypnotic effects of rhythm. At other points in the play, repeated words, phrases, rhythms and sounds add to the emotional intensity of a scene. This repetition can occur on many levels.

Repetition of words

Sometimes the same word is repeated in a short space of time in order to increase pace and tension. This is shown in the following extract from the play's dramatic opening scene:

> 'We split, we split!' – 'Farewell, my wife and children!' – 'Farewell, brother!' – 'We split, we split, we split!'

At other times, a word (such as 'loss' or 'lost') is repeated throughout a passage so that the idea can be developed or extended:

> ALONSO   You the like loss?
> PROSPERO As great to me, as late; and supportable
>   To make the dear loss have I means much weaker
>   Than you may call to comfort you; for I
>   Have lost my daughter

Repetition of sounds

Alliteration is the repetition of consonant sounds at the beginning of words:

> Foot it featly here and there,
> And sweet sprites the burden bear.

Assonance is the repetition of vowel sounds in the middle of words:

> Come unto these yellow sands,
> And then take hands

Rhyming couplets, which often end long speeches in blank verse or signal the end of a scene, also show this repetition of sound:

> Sea-nymphs hourly ring his **knell**,
> Hark, now I hear them, ding dong **bell**.

These repetitions are opportunities for actors to intensify emotional impact.

Repetition of patterns

Anaphora is the repetition of the same word at the beginning of successive sentences:

>   **Hast thou forgot**
> The foul witch Sycorax, who with age and envy
> Was grown into a hoop? **Hast thou forgot** her?

Epistrophe is the repetition of a word or phrase at the end of a series of sentences or clauses:

> Hourly joys be still **upon you!**
> Juno sings her blessings **on you** …
> Scarcity and want shall **shun you**,
> Ceres' blessing so is **on you**.

Polyptoton is repetition of words derived from the same root word, but with different endings or forms: 'Admired Miranda, / Indeed the top of admiration'.

◆ Turn to any two or three pages of *The Tempest* and identify all the ways in which Shakespeare uses repetition in those lines. Look especially at sections of Act 1 Scene 2 and Act 4 Scene 1.

◆ Try out different ways of speaking the lines to discover how emphasising or playing down the repetition can contribute to dramatic effect.

Soliloquies and asides

A **soliloquy** is a monologue – a kind of internal debate spoken by a character who is alone (or assumes he or she is alone) on stage. It gives the audience direct access to the character's mind, revealing their inner thoughts and motives. Ferdinand's soliloquy at the beginning of Act 3, as he stops carrying the logs to think about Miranda, is one example.

An **aside**, on the other hand, is a brief comment or address to the audience that gives voice to a character's inner thoughts, unheard by other characters on stage. The audience is taken into this character's confidence or can see deeper into their motivations and experiences. Asides can also be used for characters to comment on the action as it unfolds. Prospero has many asides, but his language rarely gives direct access to his thoughts. He tells stories, gives orders, comments on the action, and renounces his magic in long, spell-like speeches. Yet, unlike many of Shakespeare's other major characters – such as Hamlet or Iago – he does not have a soliloquy in which he reveals what is really on his mind.

◆ Identify some of the play's soliloquies and asides. Choose one and write notes on how you would speak it on stage to maximise its dramatic effect.

◆ Think about possible reasons why Shakespeare did not give Prospero such a soliloquy. Identify a suitable place for a soliloquy for Prospero in the play, then try your hand at writing it to reveal this character's most private thoughts.

Language and power

Throughout history, conquerors and governments have tried to suppress or eliminate the language of certain groups, defining it as 'inferior'. The ancient Greeks called anyone who did not speak Greek a 'barbarian' (speaking 'baa-baa' language). The word itself is onomatopoeic, like 'double-Dutch' or 'mumbo-jumbo', and suggests what the Greeks saw as 'nonsense' language.

In Shakespeare's time, most Europeans believed that only their own languages were civilised. Foreign languages were 'gabble', without real meaning. (Interestingly, however, it was not until the late 1300s that English was considered to be a civilised language.) The mark of savagery was not knowing English or Spanish or some other European language.

Lost words and new words

The Tempest is full of unfamiliar words that have disappeared from use today or that Shakespeare made up as he wrote the play. The meanings of unfamiliar words can sometimes be understood from their context. For example, just what are the 'Young scamels' that Caliban promises to bring to Stephano (Act 2 Scene 2, line 149)? 'Scamels' may be seagulls or clams, or may have meant something quite different in Shakespeare's time. Today, no one really knows. The word reflects the nature of *The Tempest* itself: enigmatic and not able to be tied down to a single meaning.

Furthermore, in this play of improbable happenings, Shakespeare frequently uses the hyphen to create compound words that conjure up vivid images. He puts words together to present new challenges to the imagination.

◆ Discuss what some of the following compound words might mean:

'blue-eyed' • 'brine-pits' • 'fresh-brook'
• 'hag-born' • 'hag-seed' • 'o'er-prized'
• 'over-topping' • 'sea-change' • 'sea-nymphs'
• 'sea-sorrow' • 'sea-storm' • 'side-stitches'
• 'sea-swallowed' • 'pinch-spotted'
• 'sight-outrunning'

You may notice that these words are vividly powerful, but cannot be pinned down to a single, exact meaning. Shakespeare may have used these hyphenated words because their instability expresses the sense of wonder and ever-changing reality that runs through the play.

◆ Prospero calls Caliban 'hag-seed', which means seed (child) of a witch. Make up a few hyphenated words of your own to describe Prospero or other characters of your choice.

The Tempest in performance

Performance on Shakespeare's stage

Shakespeare probably wrote *The Tempest* around 1610. Only two performances of the play are known for certain to have taken place during his lifetime – both at the court of King James. The first recorded performance was on 1 November 1611.

In Shakespeare's lifetime, *The Tempest* was almost certainly performed in two theatres: the Globe Theatre and the better-resourced Blackfriars Theatre. It seems likely that Shakespeare took full advantage of the facilities that the Blackfriars Theatre offered when he was writing the play. This indoor arena came with a group of musicians (which might explain why there is so much music in the play). It also allowed him the opportunity of using greater 'special effects' (for example, the dramatic opening storm, as well as the masque). Both theatres were owned by Shakespeare's acting company, The King's Men.

During Shakespeare's lifetime, plays in outdoor amphitheatres like the Globe were performed in broad daylight during the summer months. So, at 2 p.m. audiences would assemble with food and drink to watch a play with no lighting and no rule of silence for the audience. There were high levels of background noise and interaction during performances, and audience members were free to walk in and out of the theatre.

Shakespeare seems to want to grab his audience's attention from the very first line of the play: the storm is spectacular, and to some extent threatens to make the subsequent action something of an anti-climax. However, Shakespeare's most 'magical' of plays uses spectacle throughout: Ariel's appearance as a harpy in Act 3, the masque in Act 4, and the chasing pack of dogs in the final scene of the same act, mark this out as a play intended to 'wow' the audience.

The Tempest has music at the heart of its action: not only are there songs, but characters make reference to hearing music (In Act 1, Ferdinand talks of music creeping 'by me upon the waters', and Caliban's famous speech in Act 3 describes an island that is 'full of noises / Sounds and sweet airs, that give delight and hurt not'); and of course Stephano and Trinculo resort to drunken singing. Although all these elements certainly add to the sense that *The Tempest* was intended to be a spectacle, they also pose practical challenges for the actors on stage: for example, how do the actors deliver these lines, and how is the momentum of the plot maintained when elaborate performances are taking place?

◆ **Look at some of the most dramatic moments in the play – the opening scene, the masque, the vanishing banquet. Imagine you are the director of a school production: how would you perform these successfully? Experiment with different ways of staging these episodes, keeping in mind the themes being explored by Shakespeare in each scene.**

Shakespeare included many clues for his actors in his scripts. These clues are known as 'embedded stage directions' because of the coded instructions they give to the actors about who to talk to, when to move or gesture and when to exit. Clues about setting, weather, clothing, other characters' appearances and onstage action were also placed in the scripts. For example, in Act 1 Scene 2, we are introduced to Miranda as she is responding to the tempest that has just taken place. The dialogue that follows contains a number of embedded stage directions that help the actors establish the relationship between the two characters. What clues does Shakespeare provide the actors with in order to ensure these lines are successful? Later, in Act 2 Scene 1, the plotting pair of Sebastian and Antonio are brought to the point of killing the other courtiers, and their language is filled with coded signals, conveying meaning that only willing conspirators would receive favourably.

Embedded stage directions were incredibly valuable for early actors, because they had little time to rehearse and almost no opportunity to study the whole play before a performance. When a play was written, a scribe would make a copy. This was cut up and each actor was given a scroll with his speeches stitched together, along with basic cues and stage directions. The actors would memorise their lines, taking particular care that they knew their cues so they would be sure of when to enter and speak. A summary of the play, known as a 'backstage plot', was hung up backstage so actors would know the main story and the context for their entrances and exits. Players who knew only their parts and a plot summary relied heavily on their cues and embedded stage directions to piece together information about what was going on, who they were addressing and who was going to respond.

◆ There are many activities in the book that ask you to think about how the script should be staged. Look closely to see if there are embedded stage directions that might have been more fully developed (some examples might include Act 1 Scene 2, lines 22–87; Act 2 Scene 1, lines 1–180; Act 3 Scene 1, lines 22–98; Act 4 Scene 1, lines 195–260; and Act 5 Scene 1, line 215).

◆ Discuss with a partner what a modern director might say to actors at these points. Are all of them necessary on a modern stage? Would you consider cutting some lines if they are not necessary? How should the actors perform the lines?

This pressured system of rehearsal and performance was confusing for new actors, especially young ones, who were sometimes apprenticed to older actors while they were new to the workings of the stage. The apprentices, aged between about six and fourteen, learned the art of acting from more established actors.

In Shakespeare's day, Miranda, the spirits and Iris, Juno and Ceres were played by boys because women were not allowed to act on stage. There were no elaborate sets on the bare stage of the Globe Theatre, and even with the additional facilities of the Blackfriars Theatre, sets were limited in terms of scenery and lighting. As a result, Shakespeare included detailed and often poetic descriptions of the time and place in various scenes. Audiences needed to use their imagination to compensate for the bare stage!

However, actors wore lavish costumes, usually the fashionable dress of the times, and a range of visual and sound effects were used to add spectacle to a performance: for example, animal organs may have been used on stage, including pig's bladders filled with animal blood during murder scenes; cannon balls were rolled along tracks behind stage to simulate thunder. Storm scenes such as the opening of *The Tempest*, or the scenes on the heath in *King Lear* and *Macbeth* were probably accompanied by such sound effects. Bells, trumpets, and drums were also used, as were a range of songs, background instrumental music and dance music. The space above the stage, the upper structure known as the 'heavens', was decorated on the underside with stars and zodiac signs and used for characters to descend and ascend during a performance.

▲ In a reversal of how the play would have been performed in Shakespeare's day, this performance had women playing Prospero and Ariel.

Performance after Shakespeare

In 1667, *The Tempest* was rewritten as *The Enchanted Island.* Only one-third of Shakespeare's play was included, and a great deal was added. Caliban and Miranda were given sisters. A male character – Hippolito, Duke of Mantua – appeared. He had never seen a woman, and would be under a curse if he *did* see one. The masque and the role of Sebastian were left out entirely, although much more comedy, dance and music were inserted. Expensive stage machinery created spectacular effects, particularly in the storm scene and in the flying of Ariel and the other spirits.

This version of *The Tempest* was revived in many adaptations during the eighteenth and nineteenth centuries, with every production aiming at enthralling the audience with theatrical spectacle. One version shifted the shipwreck to the start of Act 2, so that latecomers to the theatre would not miss the elaborate stage effects contained in this scene. Another version contained thirty-two songs.

▼ **A scene from the play, published in 1857.**

These operatic and balletic versions of *The Tempest* attracted large audiences, but were often criticised for being more like pantomimes. In 1815, one famous critic, William Hazlitt, was outraged by what he saw, calling it 'travesty, caricature … vulgar and ridiculous … clap-trap sentiments … heavy tinsel'. He was tempted never to see another Shakespeare play.

▶ **This illustration shows how Caliban was portrayed in an 1850 production of *The Tempest*.**

In spite of all the criticism, the spectacular version of *The Tempest* was always popular with audiences. Each new production was hugely successful, and very profitable. It was not until the mid-nineteenth century that serious attempts were made to present the play as Shakespeare had written it.

William Charles Macready's Covent Garden production of 1838 proved a turning point in the performance history of the play. Here, the director used a script that was closer to Shakespeare's original text, cutting down dramatically on the excesses introduced in the previous century during the reign of Charles II (1660–85).

In 1897, William Poel directed an Elizabethan Stage Society production that attempted to present a version of the play that was as close as possible to the original. Twentieth-century productions – at the Old Vic and by the Royal Shakespeare Company – continued this tradition.

William Bridge-Adams's production for the RSC in 1919 staged a simple production that had at its centre the Jacobean court masque. Coming just after the end of World War I, this production – which looked back to perhaps a simpler, less destructive age – was very popular.

Later productions for the RSC, including those by Peter Brook (1957) and Clifford Williams (1978), explored the complexity of Prospero's character. John Gielgud, directed by Brook, portrayed Prospero as a rather sinister figure obsessed with his own personal demons. Williams's direction of Michael Hordern's Prospero emphasised a kinder character, but the staging – bleak and empty – showed the limitations of both his world and his power.

Derek Jacobi played Prospero in 1982. In this production, Prospero is initially motivated by a strong sense of outrage; Jacobi believed that Prospero wants 'to teach these people a lesson now they're in his power'; ultimately, though, he relents, but does not fully forgive those he has made suffer. Jacobi thought deeply about the motivation behind Prospero's actions. He said:

> I think there is a strong feeling for revenge, for the wrong that was done him, the hideous wrong that was done him. Because he was meant to die, so was the girl meant to die, and the girl was a baby. She is fifteen in the play.

> He wants to provide for her, he wants her certainly to have the future that those wicked men were going to deny her.

The actor believed that Prospero is an 'improviser': he adapts to changing conditions throughout his life, including Miranda's falling in love with Ferdinand. Such an interpretation places limitations on his power because we see that he cannot control everything.

◆ **To what extent would you agree with this view of Prospero? Does he have total control of his domain, or is he more limited – reacting to events, rather than creating them? How does such an interpretation change your view of the character and of Shakespeare's thoughts on nature?**

▼ **Derek Jacobi as Prospero in the 1982 production.**

The Tempest today

Today, most stage productions of *The Tempest* make only minor changes to Shakespeare's script, and try to avoid the sentimental escapism of earlier versions. They take the opportunities that Shakespeare provides to explore the many ambiguities and conflicts that exist in the script. Even in modern versions, however, special attention is paid to the opportunities for dramatic spectacle.

The Tempest has always been a source of inspiration for other artists, too. Mozart planned an opera based on it, but died before he could turn his plan into music. Many novelists have written 'island stories'; examples are Daniel Defoe's *Robinson Crusoe*, William Golding's *Lord of the Flies* and Marina Warner's *Indigo*. Poets have been especially attracted by the play. Shelley, T. S. Eliot and W. H. Auden all drew on *The Tempest*, and in the poem 'Caliban upon Setebos' Robert Browning made Caliban extremely eloquent and intelligent. Aldous Huxley's novel *Brave New World* imagines a horrific future society in which people are little more than robots.

The Tempest has lent itself to the shifting developments in intellectual and political thought over time. Modern productions have emphasised the postcolonial nature of the play, with Caliban increasingly presented as not only fully human, but also dignified, articulate and with a legitimate grievance against Prospero. Ariel is often portrayed as a resentful and sometimes alienated figure, preoccupied with gaining his freedom from a repressive master.

Race has featured strongly in some productions, such as Jonathan Miller's 1988 production, in which the courtiers were played by white actors and the spirits by black actors. Other productions have stressed different elements of the play: Braham Murray's 1992 production at the Royal Exchange in Manchester saw Prospero's book-lined study on set throughout the performance, and other productions have explored the charged relationship between Prospero and the sexually ambiguous Ariel. From the early eighteenth century until the 1930s, Ariel was played by a female actor.

▼ Trinculo, Caliban and Stephano in Jonathan Miller's 1988 production.

The Tempest has also proven popular with film makers, but most have taken it is a source of inspiration rather than as something to be faithfully interpreted. There were short filmed scenes made in the early twentieth century and the play was made into a BBC television series starring Michael Hordern in 1979. The Tempest has received radical interpretations by directors as diverse as Derek Jarman (Tempest, 1979) and Peter Greenaway (Prospero's Books, 1991).

Other screen and stage adaptations include the Hollywood science-fiction movie Forbidden Planet (made in 1956), and Return to the Forbidden Planet, a

1980s rock musical. More recently, in 2010 Julie Taymor directed Helen Mirren as a female Prospero (called Prospera) in a well-received film version of the play.

One of the main reasons for The Tempest's popularity with directors and actors is because the main characters can be interpreted so differently: Caliban, Ariel and Prospero are emotionally rich characters, but the themes they allow us to explore bring an additional level of complexity. Caliban in particular allows for radically different approaches from the actor and director. For much of the play's history this character was portrayed as something sub-human, and it was not

▼ The 1956 film adaptation set the story on a distant planet rather than a remote island.

until the early twentieth century that he was depicted as not only human-like but relatively civilised. The changes, of course, had occurred in society, rather than in the play itself.

Beerbohm Tree's 1904 production saw Caliban as an 'elemental man' – a figure seemingly at one with the world around him, who was becoming increasingly educated. Although his original identity was changing, it was not seen as entirely negative. This positive view of colonialism was to some extent echoed in Wilson Knight's performance of Caliban in 1938. Later productions have framed Caliban within a more overtly political context: he is seen as very much the victim of a conquering power.

Some postcolonial productions originating in former colonies of the British Empire have stressed that Caliban is exploited by the conquering European forces represented by Prospero and the shipwrecked courtiers. Not only is his land taken from him, but so too is his indigenous identity. Directors point to the exchange between Miranda and Caliban in which she tells him how she taught him to speak. Caliban's response is grudging (see Act 1 Scene 2).

Increasingly throughout the twentieth and twenty-first centuries, interpretations and productions of *The Tempest* have stressed the contrasts and conflicts between Prospero and Caliban, between colonist and native inhabitant. A 1970 production of *The Tempest* presented the play as a story of colonial exploitation. The director, Jonathan Miller, described it as 'the tragic and inevitable disintegration of more primitive culture as the result of European invasion and colonisation'. He compared Stephano and Trinculo to foreign soldiers, who patronise or bully the native population: 'they shout loudly at the people to make them understand, make them drunk and get drunk themselves'. Caliban was 'the demoralised, detribalised, dispossessed, suffering field-hand'. Miller's interpretation was in sharp contrast to the traditional image of Prospero as a benevolent ruler.

♦ **Do you think that Shakespeare's *The Tempest* is a justification of colonialism or a criticism of it – or does it not express any point of view about colonisation?**

Like many of Shakespeare's plays, *The Tempest* acts as a mirror reflecting the shifting values of society. Just as Caliban has evolved from a creature that is barely human to a figure that symbolises repressed indigenous peoples, directors and actors have drawn out different themes within the play in order to explore ideas current at the time.

The complex relationship between Prospero and his daughter has proven fertile ground for directors and actors who wish to explore the psychoanalytical aspects of the script. In some productions, the staff that Prospero wields is represented as a phallic symbol symbolising masculine dominance.

Sex, and attitudes towards it, are powerfully charged themes to explore on stage. Perhaps influenced by the work of Sigmund Freud, directors have suggested that at the heart of the father–daughter relationships (Ariel is often played by a female actor) in this play is an unconscious Elektra complex: Prospero's often angry statements are seen as a result of his inner conflict with his desire for Ariel and Miranda and an acceptance that he has to release both from his control.

Other interpretations that have drawn from psychoanalysis see Ariel as symbolic of the super-ego, with Prospero as the controlling ego and Caliban the untamed, primitive id. (You may want to spend some time researching Freudian terms and their relevance to this play, as well as to other plays by Shakespeare.)

◆ **Race and gender are often divisive issues in society and this is usually why directors are so keen to explore them on stage: they can ask searching questions of both the script and the audience's own views. In small groups, discuss how important you think the race of the actors is in this play. Think about how racial identity might change the audience's interpretation of the play's key themes.**

◆ **Consider how important the actor's gender is: what difference does it make if Prospero is female? Which male characters could easily be played by female actors, and which could not without radically changing how they are perceived? Discuss your thoughts in groups.**

The Tempest remains one of Shakespeare's most popular plays: it is regularly performed in schools (by younger and older students), and new productions by professional theatre companies appear every year. It has not only been the source of inspiration for films and musicals, but for all forms of art, including literature, manga texts, dance, songs, cartoons, blogs and fan fiction.

The play's popularity can be explained in a number of ways: it has a relatively straightforward story, complex characters, powerful themes with universal – and modern – appeal, and a sense of scale and spectacle that can entrance an audience.

Whose *The Tempest* is it?

As you have seen in the various activities in this edition, if we wish to interpret an episode in a particular way then we do so by focusing on key passages in the script. It is rare to see productions (other than those in translation) that change Shakespeare's language, but this has not always been the case.

◆ Hold a class discussion on how much freedom directors and actors should have in adapting *The Tempest*. Should every word remain untouched? Or is it permissible to cut scenes if they are not felt to be necessary (or by Shakespeare), such as the masque? Is it right to make the play overtly political? Is it possible to separate it from the society in which it is performed? Who judges such changes a success – the director, the cast, the critics, or the audience?

The Tempest on stage and on film

The Tempest is best experienced live, but if you are unable to see a production, or take part in one, then there are many different versions available to watch at home. Take time to find different versions, but remember to view each actively, rather than passively. If you are analysing a film adaptation, take notes on:

- Camerawork (angles, movement, shot type)
- Sound (dialogue, sound effects, music)
- Lighting (back light, key light)
- Editing (simple cuts, montage, fade-out shots, dissolve cuts)

For each of these points, consider what their effect is on the viewer, and how they add to (and sometimes detract from) the original script.

◆ Try reviewing different versions of *The Tempest*. You could compare and contrast two film versions, or two theatre productions. It might help to read film and theatre critics' reviews of past productions so that you can get a sense of what they focus on and of their depth of analysis. There are many radically different interpretations of this play, so remain open-minded about each.

◆ As you watch the productions, ask yourself what each is saying about its own time and culture. As you assess the various qualities of the performances you watch, think about how each differs from your own society, but also how it reflects ideas and attitudes that are still familiar today.

Posters

Promotional posters provide a 'snapshot' of a production. Their layout, typography and use of images convey the qualities of the film or play, as well as the period and culture in which they were created.

◆ Look at the posters and discuss in small groups what you think the differences between the productions might be.

◆ Stay in your groups and design your own poster to promote a production of *The Tempest* that conveys the main values of a particular community. This community could be a school, an area of a town, a financial district, or a whole society. Think carefully about the images and text you would include, and why are they relevant to *The Tempest*.

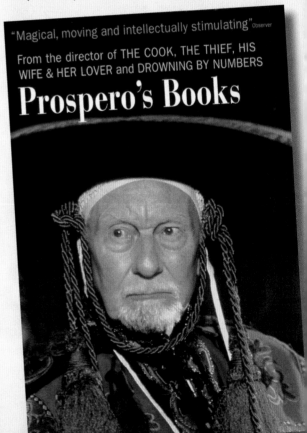

"Magical, moving and intellectually stimulating" *Observer*

From the director of THE COOK, THE THIEF, HIS WIFE & HER LOVER and DROWNING BY NUMBERS

Prospero's Books

THE
TEMPEST

by William Shakespeare

a film by

Writing about Shakespeare

The play as text

Shakespeare's plays have always been studied as literary works – as words on a page that need clarification, appreciation and discussion. When you write about the plays, you will be asked to compose short pieces and also longer, more reflective pieces like controlled assessments, examination scripts and coursework – often in the form of essays on themes and/or imagery, character studies, analyses of the structure of the play and on stagecraft. Imagery, stagecraft and character are dealt with elsewhere in this edition. Here, we concentrate on themes and structure. You might find it helpful to look at the 'Write about it' boxes on the left-hand pages throughout the play.

Themes

It is often tempting to say that the theme of a play is a single idea, like 'death' in *Hamlet*, or 'the supernatural' in *Macbeth*, or 'love' in *Romeo and Juliet*. The problem with such a simple approach is that you will miss the complexity of the plays. In *Romeo and Juliet*, for example, the play is about the relationship between love, family loyalty and constraint; it is also about the relationship of youth to age and experience; and the relationship between Romeo and Juliet is also played out against a background of enmity between two families. Between each of these ideas or concepts there are tensions. The tensions are the main focus of attention for Shakespeare and the audience; this is also how the best drama operates – by the presentation of and resolution of tension.

Look back at the 'Themes' boxes throughout the play to see if any of the activities there have given rise to information that you could use as a starting point for further writing about the themes of the specific play you are studying.

Structure

Most Shakespeare plays are in five acts, divided into scenes. These acts were not in the original scripts, but have been included in later editions to make the action more manageable, clearer and more like 'classical' structures. One way to get a sense of the structure of the whole play is to take a printed version (not this one!) and cut it up into scenes and acts, then display each scene and act, in sequence, on a wall, like this:

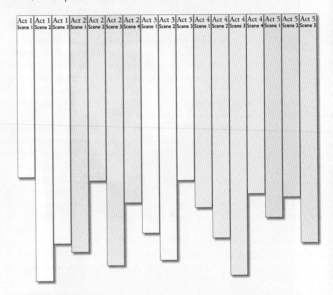

As you set out the whole play, you will be able to see the 'shape' of each act, the relative length of the scenes, and how the acts relate to each other (such as whether one act is shorter, and why that might be). You can annotate the text with comments, observations and questions. You can use a highlighter pen to mark the recurrence of certain words, images or metaphors to see at a glance where and how frequently they appear. You can also follow a particular character's progress through the play.

Such an overview of the play gives you critical perspective: you will be able to see how the parts fit together, to stand back from the play and assess its shape, and to focus on particular parts within the context of the whole. Your writing will reflect a greater awareness of the overall context as a result.

The play as script

There are different, but related, categories when we think of the play as a script for performance. These include *stagecraft* (discussed elsewhere in this edition and throughout the left-hand pages), *lighting, focus* (who are we looking at? Where is the attention of the audience?), *music and sound, props and costumes, casting, make-up, pace and rhythm,* and other *spatial relationships* (e.g. how actors move around the stage in relation to each other). If you are writing about stagecraft or performance, use the notes you have made as a result of the 'Stagecraft' activities throughout this edition of the play, as well as any information you can find about the plays in performance.

What are the key points of dispute?

Shakespeare is brilliant at capturing a number of key points of dispute in each of his plays. These are the dramatic moments where he concentrates the focus of the audience on difficult (sometimes universal) problems that the characters are facing or embodying.

First, identify these key points in the play you are studying. You can do this as a class by debating what you consider to be the key points in small groups, then discussing the long-list as a whole class, and then coming up with a short-list of what the class thinks are the most significant. (This is a good opportunity for speaking and listening work.) They are likely to be places in the play where the action or reflection is at its most intense, and which capture the complexity of themes, character, structure and performance.

Second, drill down at one of the points of contention and tension. In other words, investigate the complexity of the problem that Shakespeare has presented. What is at stake? Why is it important? Is it a problem that can be resolved, or is it an insoluble one?

Key skills in writing about Shakespeare

Here are some suggestions to help you organise your notes and develop advanced writing skills when working on Shakespeare:

- Compose the title of your writing carefully to maximise your opportunities to be creative and critical about the play. Explore the key words in your title carefully. Decide which aspect of the play – or which combination of aspects – you are focusing on.
- Create a mind map of your ideas, making connections between them.
- If appropriate, arrange your ideas into a hierarchy that shows how some themes or features of the play are 'higher' than others and can incorporate other ideas.
- Sequence your ideas so that you have a plan for writing an essay, review, story – whichever genre you are using. You might like to think about whether to put your strongest points first, in the middle, or later.
- Collect key quotations (it might help to compile this list with a partner), which you can use as evidence to support your argument.
- Compose your first draft, embedding quotations in your text as you go along.
- Revise your draft in the light of your own critical reflections and/or those of others.

The following pages focus on writing about *The Tempest* in particular.

Writing about *The Tempest*

Any kind of writing about *The Tempest* will be informed by your responses to the play. Your understanding of how characters, plot, themes, language and stagecraft are all interrelated will contribute to your unique perspective. This section will help you locate key points of entry into the play so that your writing will be engaging and original. The best way to capture your reader's attention is to take them with you on a journey of discovering a new pathway into *The Tempest*.

But first, how do you find your unique perspective? You may want to start with a character – say, Prospero. From here, allow yourself to make free connections with the rest of the play. If you think about the development of his character and the way he controls what happens on the island, this might lead you to consider his motivation and goals. Prospero's plan to isolate his enemies and confront them with their treachery points towards a plan of revenge. However, at the end of play Prospero chooses forgiveness instead of vengeance. This kind of spiritual journey is reflected in the moral development of the king and his courtiers. It is also symbolised in the tempest that follows.

You may also find yourself thinking about the way in which the play links imprisonment and freedom with forgiveness and reconciliation. The idea of forgiveness versus revenge is evident in an antithesis that Prospero uses when he decides to be merciful towards his enemies: 'The rarer action is / In virtue, than in vengeance'. This may lead you to consider the language he uses: how does it create a charmed and dream-like atmosphere? Or does he use language, along with his magic art, to control and manipulate? You might want to compare Prospero's language with the broken, strained speeches of his slave Caliban. As you do, you will notice that Caliban, too, uses some striking poetry, especially when he describes the island that means so much to him.

As you can see, your own perspective on the play will begin to develop as you think about what you are interested in and as you allow yourself to make connections between the dramatic, contextual, linguistic and thematic features of the play.

As you develop and extend your ideas into a coherent piece of writing, by using mind maps and essay plans, remember to refer back to the characters and events in the play, and to quote from the play to develop and extend your ideas further.

◆ Generate five of your own titles for writing about *The Tempest*. Try to compose your 'dream' questions that will give you plenty of scope to pull together all your ideas about the play and will take you into new and interesting areas. These could be a mixture of creative and analytical questions: be as open-minded as possible. For example, you could start with 'Ambition, power, revenge: what motivates Prospero?'

◆ Once you have five titles, work with your partner or in a small group to build up ten titles that are varied and clear, and that inspire you to write an essay in response.

Creative writing

At different times during your study of *The Tempest*, and during assessments and examinations, you will be writing about the play and about your personal responses to it. Creative responses, such as those encouraged in the activities on the left-hand pages in this book, can allow you to be as imaginative as you want. This is your chance to develop your own voice and to be adventurous as well as being sensitive to the words and images in the play.

The Tempest is a rich, multi-layered text that benefits from many different approaches, both in performance, and in writing. Don't be afraid of larger questions or implications that cannot be reduced to simple resolutions. The complex issues that have no easy answers are often the most interesting to write about.

The Tempest (the director's cut)

◆ Imagine that you are directing a movie version of *The Tempest* and the producers want it to have additional scenes. In pairs, look at each act and think about where an extra scene could be used to develop key themes. Would you add a scene that explains what life was like for Caliban and Ariel before Prospero and Miranda arrived on the island? Or would you include a scene that showed what life was like for the characters once they were back in Naples? Now choose one and write it yourself in Shakespeare's language (using iambic pentameter if you can).

◆ As part of the promotional material, the characters themselves are going to be interviewed so that they can explain their actions and give their views on the others. In pairs, write ten questions that you would like to ask the characters. Then, in small groups, conduct the interviews. If you can, film them so that the rest of the class can view them.

Essay

Some responses, such as essays, have a set structure and specific requirements. Writing an essay gives you a chance to explore your own interpretations, to use evidence that appeals to you, and to write with creativity and flair. It allows you to explore *The Tempest* from different points of view. You can approach the play from a number of critical perspectives or in relation to different themes. You can also explore the play in its social, literary, political and cultural contexts. This includes considering the range of possible effects on audiences from the play's original production (Shakespeare's day) and its ongoing reception (today or at any point since Shakespeare's day).

An essay can be seen as an exploration of the play in which you chart a path to illuminate ideas that are significant to you. It is also an argument that uses evidence and structural requirements to persuade your readers that you have an important perspective on the play. You must integrate evidence from the script into your own writing by using embedded quotations – and

by explaining the significance of each quotation and reference to the play. Some people like to remember the acronym PEA to help them here. P is the POINT you are making. E is the EVIDENCE you are taking from the script, whether it is a direct quotation, a summary of what is happening, or a reference to character, plot and themes. A is the ANALYSIS you give for using this evidence, which will reflect back on the point you are making and will contain your own personal response and original ideas.

◆ Put the following essay questions in order of difficulty (with number one being the most challenging) and discuss with others why you put them in that order. Choose one and construct a detailed essay plan that reflects the advice given in these two pages.

1 Magic in *The Tempest*: good or evil?

2 Why is Act 3 Scene 3 so dramatically effective?

3 How do the themes of transformation and self-discovery relate to Ariel's idea of a 'sea-change'?

4 Who do you think should be in control of the island? Does one character have more right to it than the others?

5 Miranda is the only female character in *The Tempest*. Why is this significant and what does her presence contribute to your understanding of other characters, events and thematic concerns?

6 Discuss the significance of the play's original context for understanding some of its themes and characters.

William Shakespeare 1564–1616

1564	Born Stratford-upon-Avon, eldest son of John and Mary Shakespeare.
1582	Marries Anne Hathaway of Shottery, near Stratford.
1583	Daughter Susanna born.
1585	Twins, son and daughter Hamnet and Judith, born.
1592	First mention of Shakespeare in London. Robert Greene, another playwright, described Shakespeare as 'an upstart crow beautified with our feathers'. Greene seems to have been jealous of Shakespeare. He mocked Shakespeare's name, calling him 'the only Shake-scene in a country' (presumably because Shakespeare was writing successful plays).
1595	Becomes a shareholder in The Lord Chamberlain's Men, an acting company that became extremely popular.
1596	Son, Hamnet, dies aged eleven.
	Father, John, granted arms (acknowledged as a gentleman).
1597	Buys New Place, the grandest house in Stratford.
1598	Acts in Ben Jonson's *Every Man in His Humour*.
1599	Globe Theatre opens on Bankside. Performances in the open air.
1601	Father, John, dies.
1603	James I grants Shakespeare's company a royal patent: The Lord Chamberlain's Men become The King's Men and play about twelve performances each year at court.
1607	Daughter Susanna marries Dr John Hall.
1608	Mother, Mary, dies.
1609	The King's Men begin performing indoors at Blackfriars Theatre.
1610	Probably returns from London to live in Stratford.
1616	Daughter Judith marries Thomas Quiney.
	Dies. Buried in Holy Trinity Church, Stratford-upon-Avon.

The plays and poems

(no one knows exactly when he wrote each play)

1589–95	*The Two Gentlemen of Verona, The Taming of the Shrew, First, Second* and *Third Parts* of *King Henry VI, Titus Andronicus, King Richard III, The Comedy of Errors, Love's Labour's Lost, A Midsummer Night's Dream, Romeo and Juliet, King Richard II* (and the long poems *Venus and Adonis* and *The Rape of Lucrece*).
1596–99	*King John, The Merchant of Venice, First* and *Second Parts* of *King Henry IV, The Merry Wives of Windsor, Much Ado About Nothing, King Henry V, Julius Caesar* (and probably the Sonnets).
1600–05	*As You Like It, Hamlet, Twelfth Night, Troilus and Cressida, Measure for Measure, Othello, All's Well That Ends Well, Timon of Athens, King Lear.*
1606–11	*Macbeth, Antony and Cleopatra, Pericles, Coriolanus, The Winter's Tale, Cymbeline,* **The Tempest**.
1613	*King Henry VIII, The Two Noble Kinsmen* (both probably with John Fletcher).
1623	Shakespeare's plays published as a collection (now called the First Folio).

Acknowledgements

Cambridge University Press would like to acknowledge the contributions made to this work by Rex Gibson.

Picture Credits

p. iii: Ninagawa Company/Barbican Theatre 1992, © Donald Cooper/Photostage; p. v: Shakespeare's Globe 2000, © Donald Cooper/Photostage; p. vi top: Shakespeare's Globe 2000, © Donald Cooper/Photostage; p. vi bottom: Dhaka Theatre, Bangladesh, Shakespeare's Globe 2012, © Donald Cooper/Photostage; p. vii top: Ninagawa Company/Barbican Theatre 1992, © Donald Cooper/Photostage; p. vii bottom: Old Vic Theatre 1988, © Donald Cooper/Photostage; p. viii top: Shakespeare's Globe 2000, © Donald Cooper/Photostage; p. viii bottom: Almeida Theatre 2000, © Donald Cooper/Photostage; p. ix left: RSC/Courtyard Theatre 2009, © Donald Cooper/Photostage; p. ix right: RSC/Royal Shakespeare Theatre 1998, © Clive Barda/ArenaPAL; p. x: RSC/Royal Shakespeare Theatre 1988, © Donald Cooper/Photostage; p. xi top: Baxter Theatre Centre (Cape Town) in association with RSC/Courtyard Theatre 2009, © Donald Cooper/Photostage; p. xi bottom: RSC/Royal Shakespeare Theatre 1993, © Donald Cooper/Photostage; p. xii top: RSC/Royal Shakespeare Theatre 1998, © Donald Cooper/Photostage; p. xii bottom: Shakespeare's Globe 2000, © Donald Cooper/Photostage; p. viii bottom: Almeida Theatre 2000, © Donald Cooper/Photostage; p. 6: Ninagawa Company/Barbican Theatre 1992, © Donald Cooper/Photostage; RSC/Royal Shakespeare Theatre 1993, © Donald Cooper/Photostage; p. 22: Theatre Royal Haymarket 2011, © Geraint Lewis; p 26: RSC/Royal Shakespeare Theatre 1998, © Donald Cooper/Photostage; p. 34: Ninagawa Company/Barbican Theatre 1992, © Donald Cooper/Photostage; p. 38: Nottingham Playhouse 2004, © Donald Cooper/Photostage; p. 43 top: RSC/Royal Shakespeare Theatre 1993, © Donald Cooper/Photostage; p. 43 bottom left: West Yorkshire Playhouse 1999, © Donald Cooper/Photostage; p. 43 bottom right: Old Vic Theatre 2010, © Geraint Lewis; p. 48: Shakespeare's Globe 2013, © Geraint Lewis; p. 52: Plan of Utopia, from Thomas More's Utopia 1518, © Topfoto; p. 54: Still from the film The Tempest 2010 © Touchstone Pictures/The Kobal Collection; p. 62: RSC/Royal Shakespeare Theatre 1993, © Donald Cooper/Photostage; p. 68: RSC/Royal Shakespeare Theatre 1998, © Donald Cooper/Photostage; p. 74: Jonathan Epstein (Stephano), Rocco Sisto (Caliban) in a Shakespeare & Company production 2012. Photo by Kevin Sprague. p. 77: Still from the film The Tempest 2010 © Touchstone Pictures/The Kobal Collection; p. 78: RSC/Royal Shakespeare Theatre 1998, © Donald Cooper/Photostage; p. 86: RSC/Royal Shakespeare Theatre 1993, © Donald Cooper/Photostage; p. 90: RSC/Royal Shakespeare Theatre 1998, © Donald Cooper/Photostage; p. 98: Old Vic Theatre 2010, © Geraint Lewis; p. 103 top left: Almeida Theatre 2000, © Donald Cooper/Photostage; p. 103 top right: Illustration from Caspar Schott's Physica Curiosa 1697, © Fortean/Topfoto; p. 203 bottom: Stephanie Hedges, Casey McShain, Jennifer Young, Monica Giordano (Spirits) in a Shakespeare & Company production 2012. Photo by Kevin Sprague; p. 106: Still from the film The Tempest 2010 © Touchstone Pictures/The Kobal Collection; p. 110: RSC/Royal Shakespeare Theatre 1993, © Donald Cooper/Photostage; p. 118: Rocco Sisto (Caliban), Jonathan Epstein (Stephano), Timothy Douglas (Trinculo) in a Shakespeare & Company production 2012. Photo by Kevin Sprague; p. 123 top: RSC/Royal Shakespeare Theatre 1988, © Donald Cooper/Photostage; p. 123 bottom: RSC/Courtyard Theatre 2009, © Geraint Lewis; p. 134: Barbican Theatre 2011, © Donald Cooper/Photostage; p. 140: RSC/Royal Shakespeare Theatre 1993, © Donald Cooper/Photostage; p. 146 top: RSC/Barbican Theatre 1983, © Donald Cooper/Photostage; p. 146 bottom left: RSC/Royal Shakespeare Theatre 1993, © Donald Cooper/Photostage; p. 146 middle right: Ninagawa Company/Barbican Theatre 1992, © Donald Cooper/Photostage; p. 146 bottom left: Rocco Sisto (Caliban), Olympia Dukakis (Prospera), Kristin Wold (Ariel) in a Shakespeare & Company production 2012. Photo by Kevin Sprague. p. 149: Theatre Royal Haymarket 2011, © Geraint Lewis; p. 150: Jericho Hands/St Giles Cripplegate 2011, © Jane Hobson/LNP/Rex Features; p. 151: Theatre Royal Bath 2012, © Geraint Lewis; p. 152: RSC/Royal Shakespeare Theatre 1998, © Donald Cooper/

Photostage; p. 153: 'Admiral Somers runs his ship ashore, Bermuda 1609' 1880, © Print Collector/HIP/Topfoto; p. 154: Sahkespeare's Globe 2013, © Geraint Lewis; p. 155: 'Roanake Landing, 1585', © The Granger Collection/Topfoto; p. 156: RSC/Courtyard Theatre 2009, © Geraint Lewis; p. 157: Open Air Theatre, Regent's Park 1996, © Donald Cooper/ Photostage; p. 158: Poster for *The Tempest* at His Majesty's Theatre c. 1920, © Michael Diamond, ArenaPAL; p. 159: RSC/Royal Shakespeare Theatre 1998, © Donald Cooper/ Photostage; 160: RSC/Royal Shakespeare Theatre 1998, © Donald Cooper/Photostage; p. 161: Merritt Janson (Miranda), Ryan Winkles (Ferdinand) in a Shakespeare & Company Production 2012. Photo by Kevin Sprague; p. 162: RSC/Royal Shakespeare Theatre 1993, © Donald Cooper/ Photostage; p. 163: Theatre Royal Bath 2012, © Geraint Lewis; p. 164: RSC/Royal Shakespeare Theatre 1998, © Donald Cooper/Photostage; p. 165: Baxter Theatre Centre (Cape Town) in association with RSC/Courtyard Theatre 2009, © Geraint Lewis; p. 166: Baxter Theatre Centre (Cape Town) in association with RSC/Courtyard

Theatre 2009, © Geraint Lewis; p. 169: Old Vic Theatre 2010, © Geraint Lewis; p. 170: Shakespeare's Globe 2000, © Donald Cooper/Photostage; p. 171: Dhaka Theatre, Bangladesh, Shakespeare's Globe 2012, © Donald Cooper/ Photostage; p. 172: Shakespeare's Globe 2000, © Donald Cooper/Photostage; p. 173 top: 'Caliban in *The Tempest*' 1850, © Topfoto; p. 173 bottom: Lithograph of a scene from *The Tempest* 1857, © 2006 Charles Walker Topfoto; p. 174: RSC/Royal Shakespeare Theatre 1982, © Donald Cooper/ Photostage; p. 175: Old Vic Theatre 1998, © Donald Cooper/ Photostage; p. 176: Poster for the film *Forbidden Planet* 1956, © MGM/The Kobal Collection; p. 177: Old Vic Theatre 2010, © Geraint Lewis; p. 178: Shakespeare's Globe 2013, © Geraint Lewis; p. 179: RSC/Royal Shakespeare Theatre 1998, © Donald Cooper/Photostage; p. 180: Poster for the film *Prospero's Books* 1991, © Moviestore Collection Ltd/ Alamy; p. 181 left: Poster for the film *The Tempest* 1979, © Moviestore Collection Ltd/Alamy; p. 181 right: Poster for the film *The Tempest* 2010, © Tempest Production/Topfoto.

Produced for Cambridge University Press by White-Thomson Publishing
+44 (0)843 208 7460
www.wtpub.co.uk

Managing editor: Sonya Newland
Designer: Kim Williams (320 Design)
Concept design: Jackie Hill